Succeeding in Healthcare Sales

Reaching the Pinnacle of the $2.7 Trillion Healthcare Industry with Applied Pyrametrics

Mark Moronell, MD

Beacon Publishing & Design, LLC
1805 Academy Drive
Anchorage, AK 99507
www.beaconmm.com
hello@beaconmm.com
phone. 907-563-6008 fax. 877-772-4093

Paperback ISBN-13: 978-0-9831644-1-8
Hardcover ISBN-13: 978-0-9831644-2-5
E-book ISBN-13: 978-0-9831644-3-2

Praise for Dr. Moronell and Succeeding in Healthcare Sales...

"Bingo! Finally someone has written the definitive guide to healthcare sales. Kudos to Dr. Moronell for filling this very important niche."

- Patrick Snow
International best-selling author of
Creating Your Own Destiny and The Affluent Entrepreneur

"A must read for anyone looking to break into one of the world's largest markets."

- Tyler Arnold
Co-Founder & CEO, SimplySocial Inc.

"I run an IT and managed services firm and am constantly looking for greater insights into the healthcare field. Mark's method is truly amazing. It is logical, powerful and it works! I highly recommend it."

- Shawn Fuller
Founder, TekMate, Inc.

"Dr. Mark Moronell has been invaluable to me and my team. He epitomizes all the traits necessary to motivate, develop and instill an unprecedented work ethic needed for individuals to succeed in a competitive economic environment."

- Oscar J. Hall, IV
Col USA (ret), Senior Director, Alaska Communications

TABLE OF CONTENTS

DEDICATION

To my parents Roberto and Ann Moronell who taught me that reaching for the stars is not just an aspiration, it's an expectation. And to my wife Tina and our children, Erin, Dana, Will and Gwen, for giving me the confidence to do it.

"In the end it is not the critic who counts or the man who points out how the strong man stumbles. The credit belongs to the man who is actually in the arena. If he fails at least he fails while daring greatly so that his place shall never be with those cold and timid souls who knew neither victory nor defeat. The joy of living is his who has the heart to demand it." - Theodore Roosevelt

INTRODUCTION

Do you want to make an impression at a networking event or a cocktail party? Tell the person who just asked what you do that you recently quit your job as a successful cardiologist to open a sales and marketing consulting firm.

I admit to enjoying the reactions I get from people. Some think I'm joking, some don't believe me and more than a couple think I'm crazy. But I'm not joking. And I don't think I'm crazy. I just see myself as one of those lucky few who get to chase a dream. After all, you only live once.

So how did I get from treating heart patients to teaching sales professionals a system that will allow them to excel in the world of healthcare sales? It wasn't a straight path. In fact, there were a lot of twists and turns along the way.

Like most people who go into medicine, I was exposed to it at a young age. My father was a psychiatrist and that was all I knew growing up. But when I was in my first year of college, he was diagnosed with cancer. This was back in the early 1980s, when treatments were not as effective as they are today. As I watched him suffer and ultimately die, I decided I didn't want to be involved in the medical field after all. Looking back that was probably an emotional decision. Nevertheless, by the time I was a sophomore, I had transferred out of pre-med and into electrical engineering.

My first job out of college was as a program manager for the United States Air Force. A few years later, I became a field sales engineer for Hewlett-Packard. The job was perfect for me – I loved selling and the freedom, flexibility and financial rewards that came with it. And as it turned out, I was pretty good at it…so good in fact that I won almost every award they offered during my five years with the company. It also transformed me from an introverted kid to a self-confident and ambitious adult.

Then one day, some college friends approached me about starting a software company. Wow, I couldn't resist the lure of entrepreneurship. And I relished the idea of being in business for myself. After all, entrepreneurship is *selling* on steroids. It was a great ride and a terrific adventure. But I never completely forgot my childhood dream of being a doctor. So one day I took the MCAT (the medical college entrance exam) and just like that, I was on my way. Ten years later I walked out a cardiologist.

Clinical medicine was immensely satisfying on a variety of levels. I loved my patients, and I truly liked and respected my colleagues. But after 11 years, things changed a lot. I became very frustrated with practicing medicine in today's economic and legal environment, so much so that I was ready for yet another change. Fortunately, a series of serendipitous events brought me to the point where I could merge everything that was important to me: medicine, technology, entrepreneurship, sales and yes, even engineering.

The result is Health Comm Strategies, a specialized consulting firm serving clients focusing on selling products and services to the vast healthcare industry. I developed the concept of Pyrametrics, a unique analytical approach to selling that provides healthcare sales professionals with the tools they need to reach their goals and have a great time doing it. As I watched the performance of my clients' sales teams climb as they learned and applied the Pyrametrics principles, I realized I wanted to share this information with a wider audience.

Thanks for being a part of that audience.

Mark W. Moronell, MD FACC

FOREWORD

by Larry Grossman

Mark Moronell was introduced to me by a mutual friend some time ago. I have been retired for a few years now and I spend my time volunteering as President of my local SCORE Chapter. SCORE is a national organization that mentors entrepreneurs. I personally have been a serial entrepreneur my whole life. After graduating college, I was able to get a great job working for a national medical equipment leasing company. I first started out as a salesman and then was promoted to Regional Sales Manager and then finally promoted to National Sales Manager. I was making very good money when I decided to quit my job and go off on my own to follow my entrepreneurial dreams. I founded 4 companies, the first being my own medical equipment leasing company that I took public through an IPO on the NASDAQ. I eventually sold the company and decided to leave the medical equipment leasing world to become the "Great American Inventor".

With some help from 3 NASA astrophysicists, I invented the Orthopedic Mini C-Arm X-Ray Imaging technology. I founded the first Mini C-Arm company and took that company public through an IPO on the NASDAQ.

I eventually sold that company and left the Mini C-Arm business. I then founded a Venture Capital Company. I ran that for many years and had several successful investments. I then decided to close down that investment fund and go back into the Mini C-Arm business. I then developed a second generation Mini C-Arm that was the first completely Digital and High Definition Fluoroscopic X-Ray Machine ever invented. I eventually sold that company successfully and retired.

The point of all of this is that every time I told my friends and family what I was going to do, they thought I was "joking, crazy or they just didn't believe me". Somehow, through sheer determination and perseverance, I succeeded much to their surprise. When I met Mark, guess what, his story paralleled mine and to say the least I was intrigued. I started out in the medical equipment leasing business, because that's what my father had done before me, so it became my childhood dream. Mark became a medical doctor because that is what his father had done and it became his childhood dream. However, as we grew in our business lives, we both became to understand that we wanted more out of life and our business careers.

We both relished the idea of being entrepreneurs and in business for ourselves. After all, America was built by the entrepreneurial spirit. We both faced many "twists and turns", but like the best roller coasters, we always hung on tight and it has always turned out to be an exhilarating ride. As we all know, the lottery tells us that you can't win if you don't play. The same is true for leaving an established, successful business where you are making a good living to journey out into the unknown abyss. By the way, we both did so with a wife and kids at home to clothe, feed and shelter. It feels like jumping off a bridge into the water below and hope you don't need a safety net to prevent your death. It's sink or swim and swimming is definitely preferable.

As a wise man once told me, "go big or go home". If we failed, going home probably wasn't the best option. We had to succeed. You always need to keep reminding yourself that you can't be successful unless you take a chance on being a failure. To be successful is all about having skill, luck, attitude and taking that "leap of faith". That is what this book is all about.

My father once told me when I was leaving home for college, "the only advice I will give you is that you first have to listen to what they want and then if you ask enough of them, sometimes they will say yes. If you don't ask, you will never get what you want". I thought he was only talking about college girls. However, looking back at it now, he was talking about everything in life and business and especially in sales.

How does this relate to the book you are about to read? Well, in this book, you will learn about Mark's "Pyrametrics Principal". You will learn about this unique analytical approach to selling to the medical professional. You will learn how and when to apply the sales tools they need to reach their goal. By using this approach, you will be able to obtain your goal and close the sale. Staying focused on the final goal is the key to great sales success.

In every successful business, you need to have a great sales team and approach the customer with the products and services that they desire. A great sales person needs to have the right attitude, ask the right questions and needs to be able to listen to what the customer has to say. Then, you need to give them what they want in order to "close the sale".

I started out my career in sales to the medical profession working for a large American Stock Exchange listed company. They did not have an effective sales training program. I had no formal training and had to learn it all from scratch. It took me several years to perfect my sales approach and even then I wasn't as effective as I wanted to be. Years later, I sold my own medical equipment leasing company to a multibillion dollar company. I soon realized they didn't have an effective sales training program in place either. Later, I sold my first Mini C-arm company to a billion dollar company. Guess what? They didn't have an effective sales training program either. I sold my second Mini C-arm company to another billion dollar company. You guessed it. They didn't have an effective sales training program either.

Now, you are about to discover that there is finally a proven and effective method to train medical sales people. You will find this knowledge in the pages ahead. I always knew there had to be a "better way" to learn how to sell effectively to the medical professional. The search has finally ended. Mark is now offering you the ability to learn the "better way" through this book and his unique approach to sales training techniques. Finally, there is an effective sales training method available to increase your ability to sell effectively to the medical professional.

When Mark first approached me about this book and his new sales training methods, I was amazed. I have dealt with all types of medical manufactures and suppliers, both large and small. None of them had a very good training program for their sales force. They all gave their sales people a "baptism by fire", and sent them on their way. Webster defines this as "A phrase that describes an employee that is learning something the hard way, like being immersed in their field of employment without proper training." Now, by implementing the ideas and methods described in this book, you will be properly trained. Your degree of sales success will be much higher and your failure rate will be much lower. You will also have more fun and enjoy your job much more. Isn't that what we all strive for?

So, please read this book slowly and in great detail. Take notes and jot down comments. Take your mind back to your school days and remember that what you learn from this book may be the difference between your ultimate success and your failure. Doesn't that make it worth your time and effort to read this?

ENJOY and LEARN!

Larry Grossman
Serial Entrepreneur
Former Founder, Chairman and CEO of:
Trans Leasing International; FluoroScan Imaging Systems; Thunderbolt Capital Co. and OrthoScan Mini C-arms.

CHAPTER 1

YOUR PRESCRIPTION FOR HEALTHCARE SALES SUCCESS

"There are no shortcuts to any place worth going." - Beverly Sills

Healthcare is one of the world's fastest growing industries. It absorbs more than 10 percent of the gross domestic product of most developed nations. In the United States, healthcare expenditures are projected to soar to $3.6 trillion by 2016. While pundits discuss legislation, litigation and who ought to pay for what, savvy salespeople are focusing on how to get their share of this growing market.

As a business-to-business market segment, the healthcare industry is unique. It's a voracious consumer of goods and services, ranging from cutting-edge technology to basic janitorial supplies. Even a fraction of a percent of a market this size could be a significant chunk of business for a given company. If you're going after this lucrative market, know this: A traditional pitch of features and benefits will likely leave you shut out of a medical practice or hospital. Healthcare providers are not looking for products. Instead, they want solutions to their very complex problems. If you understand the industry and why its various elements buy, you are on the right track to becoming a trusted partner and a sales superstar.

We'll go into each of these issues in greater detail as we move along, but some of the key points that make the healthcare industry a different kind of customer include:

- Buyers are often healthcare professionals, not career purchasing agents. They're well-educated and smart, but may not be particularly skilled at evaluating products and negotiating deals. They know the result they want, but may have difficulty articulating that in a way you can understand. They are also probably trying to divide their time between delivering patient care and buying equipment, supplies and services for their organizations.
- Healthcare providers are facing tremendous financial challenges. Expenses are increasing while revenues are decreasing. Margins are tighter than ever – a trend that is going to continue for the foreseeable future.
- Each healthcare provider who sees patients needs three support people working behind the scenes to make sure everything functions as it should. These people include nurses, medical assistants, technologists, administrators, IT professionals and clerical workers.
- Most healthcare providers are at risk of not being paid for at least a portion of the services they deliver. Certain facilities, such as emergency rooms, are required by law to treat patients without regard to whether or not those patients can pay, and the losses generated by those patients can further erode profits.
- Regulatory compliance can be a complex and even contradictory nightmare. No one would argue the need for regulations that assure the safe delivery of healthcare services, but one hour of patient care can mean as much as an additional hour (or more) of paperwork, much of it required to track compliance. That puts productive time at a premium.
- The high risk of litigation and its impact on providers and healthcare operations is greater than almost any other industry. Not only are malpractice insurance premiums a major budget concern, but some providers can feel compelled to practice defensive medicine, which drives up costs across the board. For example, in the field of obstetrics and gynecology, malpractice premiums can run $250,000 or more per year – a significant expense for even very successful practices.

- Competition is stronger than ever. The battle for patients has never been fiercer, requiring providers to be increasingly creative with their service packages and marketing strategies. It's not enough to just provide excellent care; the provider has to market that care to consumers, payers and referral sources.
- Even as competition increases, the number of players is decreasing. Hospitals are realigning, merging or, in some cases, going out of business altogether. Many medical practices are merging with or being bought up by larger groups or medical centers. And some providers are simply retiring early and getting out altogether.
- As a customer group, the healthcare market spans a broad profile. Buyers range from one-person professional practices to multimillion-dollar corporations and everything in between.

Are you wondering why any sales professional would choose an industry segment with a landscape that looks more like a minefield than a garden? It's simple: In chaos and uncertainty there is always opportunity. Despite all of its idiosyncrasies and obstacles, healthcare is still one of the few segments of the economy that is growing, and that growth is forecasted to continue. Though the challenges of selling to the healthcare industry are significant, the potential rewards are greater still.

THE ESSENTIAL ROLE OF QUALIFIED HEALTHCARE SALES PROFESSIONALS

Sales reps who understand the healthcare market and have honed the skills necessary to succeed in it are critical to the industry. They meet important needs on both the selling and buying side of the equation.

On the selling side, as salespeople do in any industry, they are generating revenue for their companies and income for themselves. On the buying side, they are a vital resource for their customers. The successful reps do far more than just sell; they help their customers articulate their wants and needs, identify problems and develop solutions.

As a healthcare industry sales professional, you'll find that your customers are sophisticated, have access to information and are under pressure to educate themselves before engaging with vendors. Their wild card is time. Despite their best intentions, they often simply don't have the bandwidth to learn as much as they'd like to or should. And they will be looking to you not only for information about your products and services, but for information about the market in general and their issues specifically – even when those issues don't have a direct correlation to what you sell.

Today's high-performing sales pros aren't bothering to join the scramble of reps who are competing for the onesy-twosy sales, and low-hanging fruit. They know the fruit that's higher up may be harder to get, but it's far sweeter – and more lucrative. They also know that today's healthcare industry customers want more than just products, more than just features and benefits. They want solutions and they want the comfort and reassurance of knowing when they buy, that your solution is the best fit for them.

I can't count the number of sales reps who called on me during the 11 years I practiced clinical cardiology, but two stand out as great examples of what works and what *doesn't* work in healthcare sales.

The first was Lyle, a pharmaceutical rep of the most obnoxious order. Even today, the mere mention of his name causes me to shudder. I don't know much about his history except that he had wanted to be a physician. When I met with him, I couldn't figure out if his true mission was selling his company's products or convincing the world of the great injustice done to healthcare because he had not become an MD. He was arrogant and condescending, with no apparent interest in forming relationships with his customers or even making sales. Instead of focusing on helping me provide better care for my patients, he spent all his time expressing disdain for the pharmaceutical industry and all the people in it. When I asked him questions about his products, his responses bordered on becoming confrontational. His tenure at our facility (and I suspect in pharmaceutical sales) was unsuccessful and short-lived.

Contrast Lyle with Beth. Beth was also a pharmaceutical rep – and that was about all she had in common with Lyle. She was a total professional, always prepared, respectful without being subservient, and willing to help us even when her efforts weren't directly related to a sale. Her exceptional ability to synthesize information she garnered from other physicians, her company and the industry in general and then show me how to apply her knowledge to my practice delivered incalculable value and insight. Because her clear priority was the best interest of my practice and my patients, I was always willing to take her calls. Even now, years later, I still appreciate her consistent professionalism. If there was a Hall of Fame for sales reps, she would be in it.

THE POWER OF PYRAMETRICS

When you understand what your customers need and why they buy, your job of guiding them to the best purchasing decision becomes easier. However, your customers' buying motivations may have little, if anything, to do with their needs. You've probably heard this many times before: People buy based on emotion then justify their decision with logic. That means that your customers buy things they *want* and, if they have to, figure out a way to justify the purchase by matching it to a need – a need that may or may not actually exist. While this is primarily true with discretionary goods such as luxury items, the activity also carries over into the business world.

Customers in the healthcare industry often *want* a lot of things, and for a variety of reasons like keeping up with the competition, adhering to new rules and regulations and as means to attain greater freedom, flexibility and earning potential. In reality, many simply do not know what they actually *need*. They often sense that something is missing in a specific area, but they don't know for sure what it is, how to get it or how much it's going to cost. They may be amazingly skilled healthcare providers, but they are in over their heads when it comes to the business side of the operation. Your mission is to adequately sort out wants from needs.

When I was in medical school, there were exactly zero hours dedicated to the business side of healthcare and it didn't get much better after graduation. For decades business principles were scorned by physicians and much of the industry as somehow beneath consideration. Take my father for example, an old-school physician whom I loved and respected dearly, he couldn't read a financial statement, thought marketing was best left to shylocks and hustlers and rarely, if ever, paid attention the bottom line. Despite all that he still did very well, because you could get away with it back then. But not anymore.

Although perceptions are changing, the changes are not coming fast enough. Your customers know they're drowning, but they can't swim and they're just hoping someone will throw them a life preserver.

That said, there are problems occurring in the vendor community as well. Even with all the allure of the healthcare market, there is a dark side to contend with. Competition is fierce and as a result margins are being squeezed across the board. Reimbursements are continuing to drop as providers and hospitals alike scramble to maintain their solvency. There is just no gold at the end of the rainbow. Companies are being forced to sell more for less and as they do, sales forces like yours are facing even greater and more pressing challenges. It is quite possible, therefore, as you're faced with more tasks than time, you too could be drowning and in need of a life preserver.

Pyrametrics is that life preserver. It is a creation that has been decades in the making and a direct result of my experience in sales, management, engineering and clinical medicine. It's the tool that will allow you to rescue your customers by empowering you to help them make sound purchasing decisions from which you'll both benefit substantially.

Pyrametrics, as the term implies, is derived from *pyramid*, a structure with a strong, broad base that rises to a focused pinnacle, and *metrics*, which are standards for quantitative assessment and measurement. Applied to healthcare sales, Pyrametrics is the process of taking a simplified approach to account management that has until now, been complicated by the sheer volume of tasks and responsibilities and reducing it to only those fundamental activities that really make a difference. And then it provides you with the most efficient means to get those activities done.

The concept was something I was introduced to as an engineering student. There it began by first adopting the mindset that any project, regardless of how complex or challenging, can be made easier if it is first broken down into its component parts. In other words, begin with the broad and complex, then move toward the focused and simple. From that point on it is matter of tackling the issues one by one until the entire problem is completed.

Amazingly the format which I now teach throughout the industry crystallized when I saw *Moneyball.* The film (adapted from the book, *Moneyball: the Art of Winning an Unfair Game*, by Michael Lewis) is based on the Oakland Athletics baseball team's 2002 season. It tells the story of how Billy Beane, the team's general manager played by Brad Pitt, assembled a record-breaking roster on an amazingly limited budget. Instead of going after the high-priced star players, Beane took it down to the basics:

- What is the goal? To win baseball games.
- What does it take to win baseball games? Scoring more runs than the opponent.
- How does a team score? By getting players on base.

So Beane looked for players who were good at getting on base. Not the great home run hitters, not even particularly strong position players, but players who could consistently get on base and push the players in front of them home to score. Those players were available at salaries the ball club could afford, and the team Beane assembled set an American League record of winning 20 consecutive games and made it to the postseason. This was an amazing accomplishment given the circumstances.

Now, how does this work in healthcare sales? Because Pyrametrics is all about simplifying the sales process, let's start with the basics:

What is the goal of healthcare sales? To efficiently and effectively sell products and services that will solve customer problems and establish you as their trusted advisor.

What is the most efficient way to make this happen? By following a process that lets you focus on the relevant aspects of selling while disregarding the myriad of other activities that just waste time.

Therefore, Pyrametrics teaches that when it comes to healthcare sales (regardless of what you are selling) there are three, and only three, activities that you should be doing each and every day. They are:

- Learning about your customer, their market and their environment.
- Educating your customer about your unique solutions.
- Building rapport and relationships with your customer.

Graphically, this process can be represented as follows:

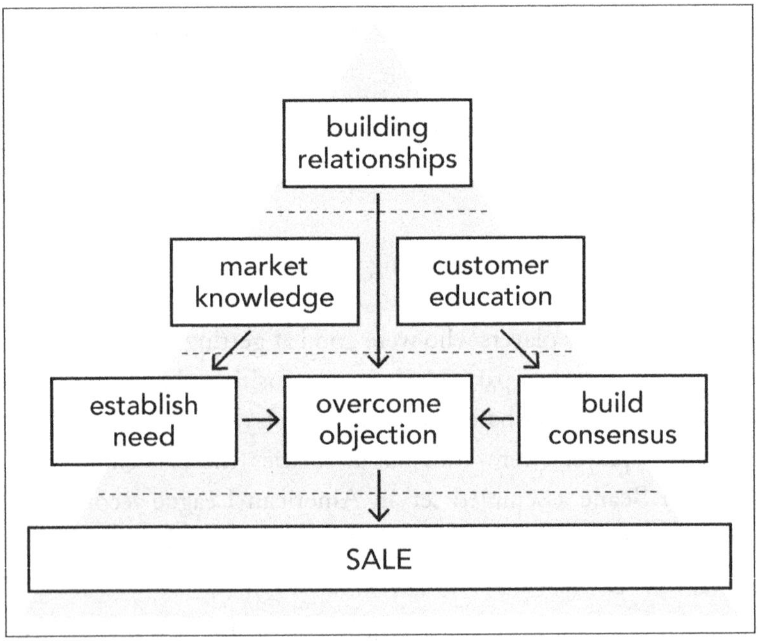

Process Management Algorithm

As you can see from the diagram this is how Pyrametrics begins to take shape. All of the activities are positioned in such a way as to support the ultimate goal - making the sale. Therefore, just as learning about your customers is the key first step toward establishing need, educating your customers is the precursor to building consensus and developing relationships is the essential ingredient that, when combined with the other two, enables you to overcome objection and move to the close. Remember the engineering mindset that was laid out above - every complex task can be made manageable if first broken down into its component parts.

A CALL TO ACTION

In the pages that follow you will learn all about the Pyrametrics process and how to apply it to your sales situations. You will learn all about your most influential future customers; physicians, hospital administrators and other healthcare providers. You will become familiar with their training, the rigors of their environment and the situations that influence their thinking and behavior. You will learn how healthcare is delivered and the differences in specialties, practice settings and employment models. You will learn who does the buying and why.

But it won't stop there. You will also learn about hospitals, hospital systems, imaging & surgical centers as well as government, military, academic and other key institutions on the front lines of patient care. You will learn not only how to assess your opportunities, but also to research your prospects, understand your accounts, decode customer behavior and ask relevant questions to obtain key information. Lastly, you will learn to be efficient with your time and resources. You will learn to set a goal, formulate a plan and then execute, not stopping until you've achieved success. In short, you will learn to differentiate yourself from the competition and in doing so you will excel in all things critical to healthcare sales success.

I hope you're ready to suit up because Pyrametrics is the game changer. It's powerful and comprehensive yet easy to implement and it's just what you've been waiting for. It's your prescription for healthcare sales success.

All that's left is for you to harness its full potential.

CHAPTER 2

LEARNING THE LANDSCAPE

"The more you sweat in training, the less you bleed in battle."
- Chinese proverb

If you recall from the previous chapter, applying Pyrametrics begins with first adopting the mindset that every challenging and complex project can be made manageable if first broken down into its component parts then tackled individually. When it comes to healthcare sales there are three things, and three things only, that you should be doing. They are:

- Learning about your customer, their market and their environment.
- Educating your customer about your unique solutions.
- Building a rapport and relationship with your customers.

As an industry, healthcare has one of the most (if not the most) diverse customer bases. If you are going to be successful in selling to this industry then you need to learn all about it. Regardless of what you sell, your customers may range from a small solo medical practice to a huge multi-location hospital system, from a busy patient treatment center to a research facility where the only "patients" are simulators or lab animals, from a high-end specialty service provider to a free basic care facility. And each type of customer will have its own culture, buying motivations and purchasing procedures.

Understanding who your customers are, how they operate and who they serve is an essential part of applying Pyrametrics to your sales process from three critical perspectives:

1. It allows you to build effective relationships that differentiate you from your competitors.

When it comes to sales there are many talented, dedicated and hardworking people out there trying to do what you do better than you're doing it. Because your customers are constantly being inundated with demands on their time and attention, it's essential for you to figure out how to stand out from the crowd. How you go about differentiating yourself will set the foundation for everything else you do in your sales career. Remember, when given a choice, customers prefer to buy from people they know, like and trust. Pyrametrics teaches that once you are able to differentiate yourself on those grounds, you can differentiate your company and finally your products and services.

2. It allows you to uncover the specific wants and needs of each customer so you can craft relevant messages they will perceive as adding value.

At nearly every moment in our lives we are faced with choices. In the end, what we decide is all about value. Your customers are no different. Therefore, when given a choice of what vendors they'll entertain ninety-nine times out of a hundred they'll choose the one that adds the most value. Taking the time to learn about your customers' needs not only adds value to their day, it also demonstrates respect which will go a long way in helping you differentiate yourself from the masses.

3. It helps you identify the revenue potential of various customer categories so you can make sound decisions on where to invest your time and energy.

Pyrametrics is all about efficiency and using your time for maximum benefit. Sometimes that involves making tough choices about how you'll spend your time and what customers you'll call on. A fundamental maxim of sales is the

80-20 Rule. Simply stated, you'll get 80% of your business from 20% of your customers. And it is that 20% that you should be focusing on. Taking the time upfront to learn about your customers will help you differentiate the most lucrative opportunities from the ones that will monopolize your time with little reward.

Now let's take a look at each type of customer and its operation. As you read this, consider why the information is being presented. Differentiation means setting yourself apart from the competition. And nothing will help you do that better than demonstrating a knowledge of your industry and your customers. In Chapter 3, we'll discuss what they buy and why.

HOSPITALS

As a group, hospitals are one of the most visible customer types for healthcare sales professionals. Even small hospitals can be big accounts, although the number of small hospitals is shrinking due to mergers and acquisitions or simply closing. But of course, the bigger the hospital (or hospital group), the bigger the amount of potential business is for a supplier.

The simple definition of a hospital is an institution which provides medical and surgical treatment and nursing care for sick or injured people. Granted, as with just about everything related to healthcare, what you need to know about hospitals is not that simple. Therefore, as you begin, keep Pyrametrics in mind. Start by developing a broad understanding of the industry and then move to the specifics of your particular market.

First, you should understand the different types of hospitals, which are:

General (community): This is the most common type of hospital facility; it is designed to treat patients with common diseases and is often the first line of care within a particular area.

District (tertiary): This is a major healthcare center (sometimes the only one) serving a particular area. Because of their higher level of care capabilities (trauma, intensive care, cardiac, maternity, burn, etc.), these facilities often receive the more complex patients and those transferred from other institutions.

Specialized: These are hospitals designed to care for unique medical issues (cardiac, cancer, burn, psychiatric) or particular patient groups (children, geriatric, women).

Academic: These hospitals are affiliated with colleges or universities; one of their primary missions is to provide education to medical professionals in training. They are often heavily involved with research and can be on the cutting edge for many new and innovative therapies.

Government: These are hospitals owned and operated by a government entity that serve a specific patient demographic, such as active duty military, veterans and Native Americans. Depending on their capabilities, they can be small, medium or large-sized institutions.

Hospital Group: These are large healthcare corporations that own/operate many different facilities under their umbrella. Examples include Providence, HCA, Banner Health, etc.

Though the types of hospitals operate differently based on their mission and market, most hospital executives agree that the three most important challenges they face in today's environment are:

1. Attracting and retaining quality providers (doctors) into their networks.

The relationship between hospitals and providers is at best symbiotic. Providers need places to treat their patients and hospitals need providers to bring in patients. Hospitals would not exist without providers and providers could do very little for their patients without hospitals. In spite of this mutual need, hospitals and providers are often fierce competitors. Many providers are equipping their facilities to deliver services in their offices that were formerly available only in a hospital setting although changes in reimbursement are curtailing some of these activities in certain markets. And many hospitals are continuing to offer out-patient treatments as part of their service as well.

2. Maintaining and improving their position in increasingly competitive markets.

Hospitals need patients and it's rare to find a hospital that is not competing with at least one other facility (and usually more) for patients. Patients come to hospitals by three routes: direct referrals from providers; insurance company mandates; and independent patient selection. That's why hospitals need to build strong relationships with providers, negotiate agreements that are beneficial to insurers, and aggressively market to the general public in their respective catchman areas.

3. Remain financially viable despite increasing costs and declining revenue.

To stay in business, hospitals must meet certain economic obligations. They have to generate enough income to stay up-to-date on technology and equipment, maintain their facilities, pay their staff and stay competitive. As the cost of providing care climbs, the income that care generates is dropping. In most hospitals, not every department is profitable, and not every activity within individual departments is profitable, either. Even so, hospitals must provide comprehensive care for all patients. Hospital executives are continuously challenged with finding the right balance between offering services that generate sufficient revenue and those that don't without impacting overall quality. Many of the more lucrative departments, such as radiology, cardiology, surgery and gastroenterology, help support the cost of other departments that tend to be less lucrative, such as the emergency room, pediatrics and general (internal) medicine.

PROFESSIONAL & TECHNICAL FEES

Because so many decisions in healthcare are affected by the reimbursement climate, understanding how providers get paid is an essential part of your preparation. Many of the decisions your customers make regarding operations, service line offerings, capital equipment purchases, partnerships and staffing are directly related to their reimbursement model. Although a complete assessment of healthcare finance is beyond the scope of this book, a few words about professional and technical fees are invaluable.

Professional Fees: In general terms, professional fees are received through direct provider-patient interaction and/or by direct provider interpretation of, or participation in, imaging tests and/or other procedures.

Technical Fees: In general terms, technical fees are received by the owner of the equipment or facility performing the procedure or study. As a general rule technical fees are much higher than professional fees.

To better under the differences in these fee types, consider the following example:

You present to the XYZ Cardiology Clinic for an evaluation of chest pain. During the course of your visit you are seen by Dr. Smith who performs a thorough consultation including a history and physical examination. Following the visit he schedules you for a stress test to be performed at the group's imaging center. Upon completion of the evaluation you receive a bill with two charges. The first represents the professional fees associated with his consultation in the office and his interpretation (reading) of your stress test results. The second fee represents the technical component of the stress test; the fee arising as a result of Dr. Smith owning the equipment. If Dr. Smith had not owned the equipment but instead had sent you to the hospital for the study then you would have received a bill from the hospital representing the technical fee for their ownership of the equipment.

Understanding the difference between professional and technical fees will help you gain insight into why there is such competition between hospitals and providers. It will also enable you to frame your messages in such a way as to effectively resonate with your customers. Remember, your customers are in the healthcare business and folks in that industry are used to dealing in facts and details, not speculation. Just as they are expected to demonstrate a thorough understanding of their business, they expect the same from their vendors. Your customers will respect and value you much more highly if you can relate to their issues as they do.

Factors Driving Hospital Costs

Key factors driving up hospital costs include:

- Patients are presenting to the hospital sicker than at any time previously.
- More and more cases of obesity, diabetes, sleep apnea, heart disease, high blood pressure, coronary disease and stroke are being seen earlier than ever. In addition, patients are presenting with these diseases at younger ages.
- A significant subset of the population does not have health insurance but still need to be cared for.
- The process of delivering healthcare is relying more and more on expensive technology.
- Due to a combination of factors, including the practice of defensive medicine and patient demand, costly items, such as new imaging modalities, stress tests and diagnostic procedures, are being ordered with increasing frequency.
- Provider dissatisfaction and turnover increase recruiting and retention costs while putting additional pressure on those still practicing.

.....

Cooperation, not Competition

Hospitals are more willing to form partnerships and joint ventures than they ever have been. When the cardiology group I worked with wanted to build a catheterization lab, we had two basic choices: We could build our own freestanding facility or we could lease space from one of the hospitals and build it on the premises. A key advantage for us in having the lab in the hospital was the proximity to all the hospital's services, such as surgical support, ICU care, etc.; things that would be essential in the case a life-threatening complication. But there were also advantages to having our own facility. With such capacity we could set up and run the facility the way we wanted to as well as obtain revenues ourselves that would otherwise have gone to the hospital.

On the other hand, the hospital already had several catheterization labs and could have seen our request as a competitive intrusion onto their campus. Perhaps they did. I imagine there were some heated discussions within their boardroom just as took place in ours. In the end, what actually happened was we both gave up a little to gain a lot. We didn't have to buy the land and build everything ourselves. Both the hospital and our practice got a new state-of-the-art facility while we got the added revenue from being able to do catheterizations in our own lab (technical fees). The hospital got revenue from our lease as well as direct referrals for patients needing additional therapy and we were able to provide our patients the added security of having them in the hospital for their procedures. We set the foundation for a longterm, mutually profitable relationship that allowed both entities to control costs and provide quality patient care.

A similar opportunity for hospitals and medical groups are *ambulatory surgery centers* (ASC). ASC's are specialized facilities that provide low complexity procedures in an outpatient type atmosphere. As providers are looking at ways to retain control and increase their revenues, hospitals are becoming more willing to partner with medical groups to build these centers in an effort to retain key services and maintain relationships with providers. What a hospital might be giving up in short term revenue is exceeded by the benefit of the long term relationship with the physicians group because the doctors in the group are not going to be sending their patients to a competing facility.

Because the relationship landscape has changed dramatically, now when you have a customer that is expanding, one of the first questions you should ask is, "Are you doing this alone?" There's a strong chance a new relationship has been formed which could affect the sales process. If you understand this and work within it, you'll become a more valuable resource to your customers and your success will grow accordingly.

TRADITIONAL MEDICAL PRACTICES

To deliver their services, doctors and other healthcare providers need an entity that combines a physical place and a business structure. You'll see a number of terms used to describe those entities including practice, medical group and professional association. The differences don't stop with the names. While they may be similar, no two physicians' offices are exactly alike: Doctors don't practice the same. Their offices are organized and managed differently and their patients may differ markedly in cultural or socioeconomic conditions. Their payer mix will vary and their desire and need for your particular products and services is unique. The more you know about your customers' organization, the more successful you'll be.

There are several important types of medical practices. The most common designations you'll hear are:

- Individual or solo-practitioner: These are small practices with one primary provider.
- Groups: Practices with more than one provider are generally referred to as a group. Groups come in many shapes and sizes from two to several hundred members and may be single or multi-specialty.
- Single-Specialty Group: A group where the providers treat only one basic patient type. Examples include pediatrics, OB-GYN, Cardiology, etc.
- Multi-Specialty Group: A group where different providers see a variety of patient types. Examples may include large internal medicine clinics that see patients with lung, kidney, heart and GI problems or large surgical practices that specialize in orthopedics, general surgery and urology all under the same roof.

Practices may also be independent or owned as a part of a hospital group, larger medical practice or other corporation. Other distinctions apply as well. Medical practices typically lean in one of two directions: patient focused or procedure focused. This is not a reflection of their commitment to patient care. It has more to do with what's necessary for them to meet the requirements of their specialty. It is also a matter of personal preference. Some specialists (surgery, emergency medicine, cardiology, radiology) provide a more hands-on, tactile approach to patient care than others. For these specialists, doing procedures is a big part of their day. This lifestyle is very appealing to some. It is also indicative of some of the personality types you'll be exposed to. There will be more about that in later chapters.

Depending on the nature of the products and services you sell, knowing these different practice types is very important. The care providers at patient focused practices spend the majority of their time in consultative activities with their patients. Their offices will normally use electronic medical records (EMR) and practice management systems (PMS), but will likely not have a significant amount of test equipment or have associated imaging centers on site. Procedure focused practices may have associated imaging centers, diagnostic and specialty testing areas, and/or intra-office labs. Offices like this typically generate, disseminate and collate large amounts of image, text and lab data. These offices tend to have more sophisticated infrastructures that are supported by larger budgets. Why are their budgets larger? Because groups with their own imaging centers and test equipment benefit from the higher reimbursing technical fees than their colleagues who do not offer such services.

Of equal importance is the fact that the number of independent, physician-owned medical practices has been steadily decreasing for years. Some are being bought out by hospitals, others by large medical groups. In cardiology alone, the number of independent medical practices is dropping substantially and the trend is accelerating. One of the primary reasons for the drop is that new reimbursement regulations sharply curtail how practices can charge for imaging tests; in other words, the technical fees are being reduced. As many cardiology practices depend heavily on the technical fees for their solvency, losing these revenue streams can be catastrophic.

Not all the news is bad for everyone. Some doctors welcome the buy-out because it lets them become employees; they can just treat patients and not worry about all the issues that go along with owning a medical practice. But a greater percentage of private practitioners are doing everything they can to avoid, or at least delay, being acquired by a larger entity. If your product offers a solution that will help them maintain their independence, you're going to get their attention but only if your message is delivered properly. By knowing the kind of folks you'll be dealing with, what their motivations are, what their working environment is like and what their personality characteristics are, you will definitely be in a different league than your competition.

SPECIALTY SERVICE PROVIDERS

A combination of technological advances and market demands have driven the development of a wide range of medical specialty service providers, some which are designed to replace traditional practices, others which augment them. At the end of the day, all of these emerging models are created to meet specific needs and maximize income in the setting of markedly declining reimbursements.

Urgent Care and Walk-in Clinics

Sometimes referred to as a "doc in the box," this type of clinic is designed to provide prompt, cost effective care for non-life threatening conditions. Patients often do not have a primary care physician or their doctor isn't able to see them immediately. These clinics are typically part of a chain and are sometimes owned by hospitals or large retailers such as drug and grocery stores. They are typically open on for extended hours, often into the evening and on weekends when traditional medical practices are closed. The range of services offered varies and care is often delivered by non-physician professionals such as nurse practitioners.

Extended Care Facilities

Extended care facilities are designed to accommodate patients with long-term care issues that require a degree of in-patient care but not the full scope of care delivered by a traditional hospital. For example, an extended care facility is an option for someone who no longer requires acute hospitalization but needs extensive rehabilitation following a prolonged illness, trauma or complicated surgery. The care is sufficient to the patient's needs and can be delivered at a significantly lower cost than an academic or community hospital.

Specialty Hospitals

Specialty hospitals serve a niche patient population consisting largely of patients who require customized programs such as cancer, advanced heart disease and orthopedic issues. These facilities are generally smaller than traditional community or academic medical centers but they have the same basic infrastructure needs. You may also see extensive crossover with providers working in both places. It's not uncommon to see an overlap between extended care facilities and specialty hospitals in patient types, organization and affiliation with larger traditional hospitals and medical centers.

Boutique Hospitals

Stand-alone facilities that treat very specific health issues are operated independently, as part of chains or as divisions of larger medical centers. These specialized institutions typically treat high volume, big ticket conditions such as behavior, mental health and addiction issues, and certain types of rehabilitation.

Imaging Centers

The ability to visualize injury or disease through the use of technologies such as X-ray, computerized tomography (CT), magnetic resonance imaging (MRI), ultrasound (USN), positron emission testing (PET) or nuclear medicine is valuable from a healthcare quality perspective and lucrative from a provider prospective. Many imaging centers evolved either in partnership with hospitals or medical groups or as independently-owned entrepreneurial operations.

Partnership facilities may share policies, protocols and staff with their owner institutions, which may be helpful if you have a relationship established with the parent organization. Independent facilities may compete directly with larger hospitals and clinics, and therefore be receptive to efficiency and cost-containment solutions.

Ambulatory Surgery Centers

Similar in concept to imaging centers, ambulatory (or same-day) surgery centers and special procedure facilities have developed to capitalize on the high rate of reimbursement for more routine, lower risk surgical procedures. These entities typically perform less-complex out-patient surgeries and specialized procedures such as cosmetics, endoscopy, biopsies, and so on. Some are hospital-provider partnerships while others were established by providers who want to work independently of hospitals. These facilities can do exceptional work efficiently and cost-effectively.

The Profit Status Issue

Some of your smallest customers can be for-profit entities while some of your largest will be nonprofits. You need to recognize their differences and similarities.

Of course, the most obvious difference is that a key goal of a for-profit entity is generating profits for its owners and/or shareholders. But just because an entity is non-profit doesn't mean it isn't concerned with revenue. Also, both types of entities need to operate with the parameters of all applicable regulations regarding their legal and tax structures. And they may use different language for essentially the same activities. But goals and concerns they share include:

- Increasing revenue, whether from the sale of services or contributions from donors
- Containing or reducing costs
- Attracting and retaining high performing employees
- Improving productivity

- Delivering quality service
- Innovation
- Regulatory compliance

GOVERNMENT MEDICAL FACILITIES

Without making a political comment on the current state of flux of the healthcare industry in the United States, it's safe to say that government at all levels is a major provider of healthcare services. Public health departments (generally operated at the county level) across the country offer varying ranges of services and should be explored as prospective customers for medical sales professionals. Nationally, the two largest government medical entities are operated by the United States Department of Veterans Affairs, commonly known as the Veterans Administration or VA, and the military.

The purchasing process at these facilities may be done locally or it may be centralized at a regional or national level, depending on the product or service. For example, pharmaceuticals will likely be purchased under different protocols than those that apply to information technology, medical equipment and supplies or non-medical supplies. To make it even more challenging, the procedures for similar products may be very different; for instance, an entity may purchase certain specific software applications locally but acquire other applications through the centralized system. Be prepared for wide variations in business operation, and take the time to find out as much as you can about how the entity you'll be calling on functions before executing your sales plan.

VA Hospitals and Clinics

As perhaps the most recognizable government healthcare organization in this country, VA hospitals have received extensive media attention for both their excellence in treating our military veterans and for some less-than-excellent care, facilities and operational issues. The mission of the VA is to fulfill

President Lincoln's promise "To care for him who shall have borne the battle" by serving and honoring the men and women who are America's veterans.

The VA's healthcare system includes 153 hospitals (at least one in each state, Puerto Rico, and the District of Columbia) and more than 1,400 sites of care including 909 ambulatory and community-based outpatient clinics, 135 nursing homes, 47 residential rehabilitation treatment programs, 232 Veterans Centers and 108 comprehensive home-care programs. The VA manages the largest medical education and health professionals training program in the U.S. VA facilities are affiliated with 107 medical schools, 55 dental schools and more than 1,200 other schools across the country. VA research has earned an international reputation for excellent in areas such as aging, chronic disease, prosthetics and mental health. Special VA "centers of excellence" conduct leading-edge research in areas of prime importance to veterans, such as neurotrauma, prosthetics, spinal cord injury, hearing and vision loss, alcoholism, stroke and health care disparities.

Its size and scope means the VA is a huge customer, but it is still a government organization with all the accompanying red tape, hurdles and delays. The key to successfully selling to a VA facility is to learn its system and work within it.

Military Medical Facilities

While the VA cares for veterans, military medical facilities provide care for active duty service personnel and their dependents. Most military medical facilities are located on military installations. Some are affiliated or co-located with academic or community medical centers to provide more comprehensive services. They are staffed with a mix of civilian and active duty medical personnel, with few academicians and trainees. Like the VA, these entities are part of a large government bureaucracy with very definite – and not always logical – purchasing protocols and procedures. Take the time to learn the system before you tackle it.

ACADEMIC MEDICAL CENTERS

Academic medical centers are usually affiliated with large universities and/or government institutions. They are often located on campus and in close proximity to medical schools and other educational facilities or near government medical facilities and other research facilities.

Because of their affiliation with medical schools, academic medical centers often enjoy the status of being premier healthcare facilities. They employ many of the top and most-recognized practitioners and are the source of many new procedures and treatment protocols, equipment innovations and research studies.

In the past, academic medical centers served a unique niche: while caring for patients, they operated primarily as teaching institutions for healthcare professionals. A substantial amount of their funding came from government subsidies and research grants. However, like all other healthcare service providers, academic medical centers are being forced to adapt to a shrinking reimbursement pool and are more likely to be competing with community hospitals than they have in the past. As specific research dollars and funding grants become increasingly scarce, these institutions are responding by expanding traditional patient care activities and other sources of income. For researchers, this means balancing clinical and research work is more difficult than ever.

Medical schools and academic centers operate within a fairly strict hierarchy. Before you make your first call on an academic medical center, you should take the time to research its structure and culture, and find out where the institutional power is so you can adapt your sales process appropriately.

It's generally accepted that academic providers are not as financially driven as their non-academic colleagues might be. They are typically paid less than their independent counterparts and may be more interested in the opportunity to teach, conduct research or become involved with healthcare policy. Having students, residents and fellows around can lighten their clinical load and free up time for other pursuits. If you're to be calling on academic medical centers take the time to research the facility, the customers you'll be dealing with and the issues relevant to the industry and local markets.

Research Centers

Research laboratories typically operate as a "business within the business" of academic medical centers. They are often overseen by a research physician or a PhD in a specific field and may be funded through grants. Their systems and procedures will often vary from one laboratory to another, as well as from the rest of the institution. Some research centers have substantial budgets and purchasing authority for equipment in support of their activities; others are not as well-funded. Savvy sales professionals take the time to understand the hierarchies of the research centers and individual laboratories so they have the foundation necessary to develop winning solutions that will lead to sales.

OTHER PROVIDER TYPES

In addition to these major customer groups, every market has a wide range of other potential customers for most healthcare sales professionals. It's likely that your products and services are needed by dentists (general and various dental specialties), chiropractors, podiatrists, optometrists, psychologists, therapists, behavioral and occupational health professionals, as well as some I haven't listed.

Regardless of who you're calling on, Pyrametrics principles apply and you should always use them to your benefit. Therefore make sure to always learn as much as you can about the industry; starting with the broad and complex and moving to the specific.

WHAT THEY ALL HAVE IN COMMON

When applying Pyrametrics, you always move from the complex to the simple, from the broad to the specific. So remember the pyramid - the base is your foundation of knowledge about the overall market and the pinnacle is that knowledge applied to one specific customer. Pyrametrics is designed to help you sort out what is important in healthcare and how to apply it. Clearly there is a tremendous amount of variety in healthcare industry customers, but what they all have in common (from the smallest solo practice to the largest hospital chain) is that they're struggling under the collective burden of regulatory and economic uncertainty, increasing costs and decreasing revenue. But as mentioned before, one man's burden is another man's opportunity. Though you won't be the only sales rep calling on these healthcare accounts, you want to be the only one they remember. The sales rep who understands that and who is able to craft relevant messages that demonstrate their understanding will stand to benefit the most.

Now that you're familiar with the landscape, let's find out what's being purchased. Then we'll move on to who's doing the buying.

CHAPTER 3

KNOWING WHAT'S NEEDED

"Ambition is a dream with a V8 engine." - Elvis Presley

Just as the previous chapter introduced the value in learning about your customers, this chapter will expand on that concept even further. Applying Pyrametrics, as you recall, begins by developing an understanding of the macro-environment of healthcare. That is your foundation, your knowledge base. From there you build upon that foundation to include your specific markets and specific customers. An integral part of this process is knowing what your customers spend their money on, how that equipment is used and why it's important in the performance of their business. Unfortunately there is no shortcut to building your knowledge base, you just have to go out and get it done.

What does the healthcare industry buy? The short answer is: Just about everything except raw manufacturing materials. The healthcare industry is a major consumer of technology, from systems that support day-to-day operations, equipment necessary to deliver care and ancillary services that keep the whole process running smoothly. Providers also have plenty of low-tech needs as well.

If you're considering a career in healthcare sales, you have a wide range of opportunities to consider. If you're already in sales and looking to expand your reach, this chapter will give you some ideas of niches within the industry that you may want to target. I've also included some realworld perspectives to help you gain insight into this arena because regardless of your position, a successful sales experience is the ultimate goal. But before you can really "wow" those customers, you'll need to prepare thoroughly for each and every engagement. Pyrametrics will help you make that happen.

The Healthcare Employment Picture

The U.S. healthcare industry employs one out of every eight American workers – that's approximately 16 million jobs. A significant number of healthcare workers are professionals who hold graduate degrees, undergraduate degrees, associate degrees and various certifications. Therefore, the industry is a major consumer of education and training, including programs designed for initial and ongoing qualification. That means your customers will be some of the mostly highly trained and educated in the world. If you are going toe to toe with them, you'd better be very educated about what you're doing as well.

As a sales person you will certainly not engage with everyone of those 16 million people. But you will likely be calling on a diverse cross section of the industry nonetheless. Remember, one of the best ways to resonate with your customers is to exhibit the same qualities as they do. Healthcare customers are smart, hard working and meticulous in their execution. How you adapt to and prepare for each new demographic and respond to customers' individual needs and challenges, will demonstrate the kind of partner you are and will be a key predictor of your overall success.

IT'S ALL ABOUT PREPARATION

In the very first chapter, I mentioned that if you were planning on merely selling features and benefits to your customers that you would not be successful. I meant it. Today's healthcare market is very competitive. It is almost unimaginable that you will be the only one selling your type of product or service. Therefore, the only chance you may get to truly differentiate yourself from everyone else is at the first encounter. Pyrametrics teaches that you first must be successful in differentiating yourself, only then you can differentiate your company and, lastly, your products and services. Like the old saying goes, "*you never get a second chance to make a first impression*". So, you'd better get it right the first time.

I was directly involved in medicine for over two decades as a student, trainee, practicing cardiologist, senior partner, group VP and department chairman. In that time, I encountered sales reps from every corner of the healthcare industry. Without a doubt, the most common deficiency I saw was in their call preparation. They simply did not take the time to learn about their customers. Consequently they would come to the sales call looking for answers instead of being prepared to discuss solutions.

If you're wondering, "How can I make sure that doesn't happen to me?" Don't worry, that question will be answered formally a little later on. But for now I will tell you, as someone with experience sitting on both sides of the table, you can never be too prepared or too knowledgeable about your customers. Consider this question.

Do you know what really happened the last time you went to the doctor for a routine check up?

Although you've certainly been to the doctor for something, how much do you truly know about what happens there? If you're just going in as a patient then it probably doesn't matter much, so long as you're well cared for. But if you're both a patient AND a healthcare sales rep, it might matter a lot.

So, if you answered...

"Well, I showed up on time, filled out some paper work and then sat down for a while. Eventually the nurse came out and took me back to the room. There she asked me a few questions, typed a couple of things in the computer, listened to my chest and then made me wait some more. Finally, the doctor came in, asked me a few more questions, looked me over quickly, handed me the bill and left. I headed to the front desk, paid, got my things, made my next appointment and then took off."

... then you'd make a fine example of a typical patient but a lousy example of a healthcare sales rep who is supposed to understand the intricacies of their customer's operation so that you can discuss their needs intelligently and then offer relevant solutions.

A more impressive response would have been this...

"I entered the office at 10:10 am and checked in at the desk. There the receptionist asked for my name then queried her computer. On the screen I knew that my name had appeared from the master list of patients for that day; it verified my 10:15 am appointment with Dr. Smith. I presented my insurance card which she took then queried her computer again. The information she received listed my insurance company, what my payment terms were and what my deductible was. She also knew I had family coverage and that there was an unpaid balance from my wife's last visit for $50 (which I was unaware of). She knew who I was, who my family members were, my address, where I worked and my credit score. She then returned my card, handed me a questionnaire to fill out and then I sat down.

"A few minutes later I turned in the completed sheet. She then ran it through a scanner and the answers automatically populated into my chart in their electronic medical record (EMR) system. I waited a few more minutes until the nurse called me back to the examination room.

"In the examination room, the nurse asked me a series of additional questions which she checked off on a computer screen as I answered. I knew she was entering information into the *Review of Systems* section of the EMR. She then took my pulse, my breathing rate, weighed me, checked my height and performed a cursory examination. Once that was finished, I waited a little longer until the doctor came in to see me. I knew that before the doctor saw me that she had taken a minute to review my records on the computer, as well. She checked over the information provided by the nurse and looked through my file to see if there was any relevant information or outstanding issues from past visits. Then she cross referenced the local hospital for results like imaging or lab tests. After reviewing all of that, she came into the room and performed the examination.

"Once the visit was concluded she presented me with a sheet called the *Super Bill.* The super bill lists everything done at the visit and the charge codes for each. Every type of patient encounter has a code assigned to it and there are specific charges depending on the level of services performed. On my way out the door I handed the super bill to the front desk person who entered that into the system along with all my other information. He then asked me for my share of the deductible, collected the payment via a credit card reader and scheduled me for a follow up visit in three weeks.

"Since my doctor ordered a routine blood test, he made sure those charges were posted. I received a reminder of the testing times, a map with driving instruction to the lab and a summary of my visit; all of this was printed directly from an intra-office database. I also received verification that my prescription had been emailed to the pharmacy and received. In the mean time, I knew the system sent the appropriate charge to my insurance company for payment as many practices submit bills on behalf of their patients.

"I also knew that, more often than not, the bill is rejected by the insurance company for any number of possible reasons. I knew my doctor's office would get a denial notice and then they would automatically go through the motions of re-filing. Fortunately, their EMR and practice management systems (PMS) facilitate these transactions. In time some payment would be received, then I would get an EOB (explanation of benefits) from the insurance company and a bill from the office for the balance.

"Every few months their office administrator would review the finances and get compiled summaries of the insurance payers, their payments, accounts receivable, and much more information. They know exactly what my payment history is. In the end, they will have compiled a very detailed history of all parts of my treatment experience. This is a typical medical practice scenario that is repeated many times each day."

For someone committed to selling products and services into the healthcare sector, having a familiarity of the process in such detail is by no means unusual. Developing an understanding of your customers takes time, but is a worthy investment because in the end, very few other reps will exhibit such dedication.

TECHNOLOGY AND RELATED PRODUCTS AND SERVICES

Healthcare is a voracious consumer of technology. Hospitals and other providers need a wide range of equipment and services to deliver care and operate their businesses. Where the previous section highlighted some of these items, this section will introduce them further. As you review each item try and keep in mind Pyrametrics, why this information is being presented and how you can use it help craft relevant messages that will resonate with your customers.

Health Information Technology (HIT)

The only consistent aspects of health information technology are its complexity and propensity for change. Health information technology is a broad term that encompasses many different products and services including traditional elements like computers, monitors, printers, routers and servers, along with related technologies such as bandwidth, connectivity, smart phones, tablets and system support services like installation, maintenance, security, redundancy, back up and more. The need for hospitals and providers to access information quickly, securely and cost-effectively has never been greater. In fact, HIT has become so essential to the healthcare industry that you cannot discuss hospital or group operations at any level without mentioning its contribution.

In my old cardiology group we had a definite love-hate relationship with HIT. On one hand it was an essential component of our business that allowed us to function adequately, share data, communicate and keep our entire organization together. On the other hand, it could be frustrating, difficult to use and maintain and very expensive. During my tenure we went from employing a single consultant part time, to staffing our own 4-man department until finally outsourcing the whole kit and caboodle to a managed services firm. And at each step along the way the process became more complex and costly.

In today's healthcare environment both providers and hospitals alike are caught in a Catch-22 of sorts; HIT is not an option, it is an essential component of business whose demand is being driven as much from internal sources as external ones. Organizations need HIT to improve efficiency and reduce costs even though it remains one of the biggest expenses. Furthermore, although government monies are being made available to aid in the adoption of such systems, the funds rarely cover the full costs. Such monies take the edge off the initial investment but do little to offset the costs in later years. Therefore, once an organization takes the leap into HIT, they are committed and those costs become a recurring component of every future income statement.

If you are selling HIT, you need to empathize with your customers on this issue. Furthermore, when it comes to selling HIT, savvy reps know that in order for their message to resonate with their customers they cannot simply push features and benefits. Instead, they must first understand how HIT impacts their customers' overall operation, including their initial and long term costs, staffing requirements, ramp-up time, etc. and then position their products accordingly.

Practice Management Systems (PMS)

In the opening section, the "glue" that held the doctor's office together was their PMS. Practice management systems are essential for the optimal management of any medical group or provider's office. These are software-based tools that coordinate most activities within a medical practice and integrate them for a more efficient operation. PMS typically address functions such as appointment scheduling, billing and accounting, revenue and expense tracking, and serve to integrate all incoming patient information into one manageable repository. PMS also need to function in concert with the EMR, imaging equipment, laboratory information and other vendors' systems and they need to do it seamlessly.

One of the biggest issues many sales reps face in healthcare is the frustration felt by customers due to the ever-increasing number of vendors in the market. For example, in my cardiology practice, as part of our imaging capability, we maintained two nuclear cameras, five echocardiogram machines, one CT scanner, one MRI scanner, one X-ray machine and one stand-alone catheterization laboratory. Much of this equipment was distributed among our three offices. Not surprisingly, even as many of these items were supplied by different vendors, they still had to share information and operate as part of the overall network. Our PMS was essential in making that happen.

Obviously, the more complex the network, the more problems that arise. For us, the biggest problems arose when one device would not talk to another. At that point we never knew who to call. If we asked Vendor A why their device didn't talk with Vendor B, they'd say it was Vendor B's fault. Then you can imagine what Vendor B said in response. If you are selling into the healthcare space nowadays you will see very quickly how interdependent different products are on each other and the problems that arise when things don't work as advertised. Although PMS are designed to overcome these problems, it is a certainty that your customers will still have difficulties frequently.

What is also clear is that they don't have the time or inclination to solve these problems themselves. That's why they're looking to you. Remember, you are the face of your company. You are the first person a customer thinks about when problems occur. A key opportunity for differentiation is to recognize these problems at the outset and address them *before* your customers do. This will help develop your excellent reputation.

Billing and Collections Systems

Getting reimbursed (or paid), regardless of the payers involved, continues to be a source of stress and frustration for providers. Bureaucratic government agencies, resistant insurance companies and cash-strapped individuals all create their own special obstacles to receiving timely payments. This has spawned the development software products designed to facilitate these transactions and maximize reimbursement potential. Some billing and collections programs are stand-alone products; others are part of an integrated practice management system and some companies offer these services in a completely out-sourced model. Either way, they are essential to the operation of most practices.

The issue of reimbursement is paramount in healthcare. And because of the dysfunctional and conflicting payment systems in this country it can be time consuming and costly for your customers to get paid. Here is an example. When you go to the doctor, and assuming you have insurance, some (but likely not all) of your bill for that visit is paid by the insurance company. The remainder is your responsibility. For most practices that means they have to send out two bills - one (or sometimes more) to the insurance company on your behalf and the other to you for the difference. Because the process is fragmented, it can take 60 to 90 days, or longer, for them to get paid. This type of delay can strain any cash flow situation. Furthermore, as a byproduct of the poor economy, many individuals are taking longer to pay their share of the medical bills if they even pay it at all; many simply don't. As a result, for many practices the amount of lost revenue continues to grow. This is a source of substantial stress.

Now, if you're a Medicare patient, the situation can be even more troubling for the provider. Medicare rarely pays the full cost of an office visit; a fact that is forcing many providers to no longer accept Medicare patients. Medicare also forbids the provider from *balance billing*, or billing you for the difference, like they can do for privately insured patients. The result is that while a provider may charge a Medicare patient $100 for a visit, they only get reimbursed about $45. In addition, they are not allowed to balance bill for the remaining $55; nor can they take that $55 as a write off loss on their taxes. These are but a few of the reasons many practices are in such trouble. This is also why products and service that help address these problems are so popular.

The reason this information is being presented is so that you can better understand what billing and collection companies do and also take into account the overall environment when deciding how to position your products. I can assure you, if you are able to demonstrate to your medical customers an understanding of why their reimbursement situation is so tenuous and then introduce your products in such a way as to alleviate this tension, you will resonate with them on a much higher and more personal level. Understanding builds strong bonds with your customers and differentiates you from the myriad of others who cannot, or will not, take the time to do the same.

Electronic Medical Records (EMR)

Electronic medical records (EMR), also referred to as electronic health records (EHR), were developed as an alternative to the paper-based patient records or charts. When fully integrated into a practice, EMR systems contain the same information paper records do but with enhanced accessibility, readability and redundancy. Also, as reimbursements are tied to having proper information documented at each patient encounter, EMR systems offer platforms to ensure proper data compliance and maximization of revenues.

New government mandates continue to refine the standards from which EMR systems are evaluated. In general, EMR systems must provide 24/7 functionality and connectivity with other systems - including the ability to input and export data from many sources; like pharmacies (e-prescribing), other providers' offices and independent hospitals. And because providers are increasingly mobile, EMR systems must be accessible from anywhere; including home, office and while the user is in transit.

Several years after their introduction into the market we are still seeing a lot of debate and controversy about the performance, cost, value and ROI of these systems, but in the final analysis, they are here to stay. Even if you do not specifically sell an EMR product, you'll find that it's difficult, if not impossible, to discuss any hospital or group operation without considering this technology and its impact on the customer. Therefore, you'd better develop at least a working knowledge about these systems because they will come up in conversation.

During my time in practice I was involved with three EMRs. The larger hospital in town introduced one and my group rolled out two systems over the period of about six years. The first cost around $500,000, the second, over $1,000,000. Sure, there definitely were some benefits to having those systems in place. When they were working well I was able to access information quickly and efficiently and from many different places. In the final analysis though it is hard to determine whether or not we broke even on either one because there were so many associated costs.

One of the hidden costs that you rarely hear about is the cost of having to change routines. From the first days of training providers learn a routine and they maintain that routine because it is familiar, efficient and productive. Think of it in terms of what you do when you first wake up in the morning - you roll out of bed, brush your teeth, take a shower, get dressed, have breakfast and go to work. OK, now think of how disturbing it would be to have that routine jumbled, especially if you have been doing it the same way for years.

As a cardiologist I could see a new patient in the office, examine them, write the orders and dictate their note in under thirty minutes. I had a routine that was fast and efficient and it let me get my work done and not miss anything. When the group introduced the new EMR it blew my routine to pieces. The time it took me to do those very same things doubled. In medicine you only generate income through patient encounters. Therefore, since it suddenly took double the time to see the same number of patients then either I was going to have to work twice as long (not an option) or try and speed up, possibly cut a few corners and probably put my patients at risk (also not an option). Either way, the stress was terrible. We responded by hiring more people to help work around the problems. Sometimes it was successful, sometimes it wasn't. But it certainly raised the cost of doing business.

When a hospital or group commits to rolling out an EMR they must be all in, because you just can't go half way. This can cause substantial upheaval in any organization. Even though many things about EMRs are still being debated, the issue of whether or not they disrupt existing routines, at least for some period of time, is not one of them. They do.

What I've just described, is happening throughout healthcare and regardless of where your customers are this is an issue for them. At the end of the day, the concept of using computerized patient records is sound and EMRs are actually very good products. However, until all the bugs are worked out there will be continued uncertainty and stress. If you are in healthcare sales, you need to understand this. And you need to work diligently to help your customers understand this too. Remember, they are investing a lot, in both time and money, in these new systems. They are expecting to see some ROI and will be looking to you to help guide them.

Diagnostic Imaging and Laboratory Equipment

Imaging equipment is a huge industry. CT scanners, ultrasound, X ray, MRI, endoscopy, fluoroscopy, nuclear medicine, PET scanning, etc. The list goes on and on. Medical facilities also need specialized laboratory equipment from the most basic electrolyte panels, pregnancy tests and blood counts to sophisticated disease screening and monitoring studies. The dependency on these products for patient care is huge. Furthermore, those who own the actual equipment benefit from the increased revenue generated through owning the equipment for which the equipment is used (technical fees). For that reason alone these products will remain in demand for the foreseeable future.

This was alluded to previously but I'm mentioning it again because it is such a timely issue. Both independent practices and hospitals alike are suffering from continued reimbursement cuts and therefore depend highly on diagnostic and laboratory equipment to supplement their revenue streams. In many cases the income generated from these products makes the difference between whether a medical practice remains independent, has to merge with another entity or sell out completely. This is a really big deal. If you're wondering why, I will try to explain.

In addition to wanting to care for patients, most providers, not all but most, went into medicine for the independence. They did not want to be part of a big organization, to fall into some org chart or to have a boss to report to. They went into the profession to be small business owners, to do things their own way and to be in control. Those were some of the perks that a career in medicine offered.

Now however, the current trends in healthcare are turning this reality upside down and that has many providers unhappy. In fact, morale is now at all time low. It is also impacting how care is delivered. I'm including this information not to make a political statement. The situation is what it is. There are many who think these changes are long overdue. There are many who don't. Regardless of who thinks what, the only certainty is that the new reality will be different from the existing one.

As a sales person, your job is to sell. But in order to sell effectively you must know what is going on in the industry and be able to relate to it. If you're selling imaging or laboratory equipment, these issues will come up in conversation. I guarantee it. It's up to you how to respond to it. My advice is take this information for what it's worth and remember that chaos for some means opportunity for others. Use this uncertainty to your advantage by demonstrating empathy for your customers. In the end they will look to you as a partner and a friend.

Biotechnology and Other Specialized Equipment

Most medical specialties require a range of devices to treat their unique diseases and help restore function. Some of the more recognizable examples of these devices include pacemakers, defibrillators, stents, artificial joints and prostheses. Some of the specialized equipment includes surgical gear, monitoring equipment or safety products. This type of selling can be particularly rewarding as many of these vendors actually accompany their customers into the operating rooms, intensive care units and clinics where these products are placed. In addition to calling on providers, it's common for reps selling these products to have frequent patient encounters as well.

Healthcare personnel care very deeply about their patients. So if you ever have occasion to interact with patients then you had better demonstrate a similar commitment. To put it bluntly, no one really gives a hoot about you or your products. They only care about what you and your products can do for their patients. Recognizing this and adopting the proper attitude will only help you in the long run. Remember, feature and benefit selling to the healthcare industry is not going work, not any more. There are just too many competitors out there. That is why you must always position your products in terms of meeting a need or solving a problem. When it comes to this industry, there is no bigger need than patient care.

PHARMACEUTICALS

Perhaps the best known and most-maligned area of healthcare sales is pharmaceuticals. Over the years they have gotten themselves in hot water with questionable sales tactics and overzealous reps. In recent years however, the industry has really made the effort to sharpen their image.

The pharmaceutical industry, though very profitable, has its share of difficulties. Drug manufacturers are continuously challenged by the time and resources required for product development. Often the development timeline can be a decade or longer. Once a product makes it to market, companies have only a relatively brief window of opportunity to recoup costs and recognize profits before protective patents expire and the product goes generic.

The pharmaceutical industry has undergone a significant contraction in recent years due to a near-perfect storm of government regulations, more products going generic and restrictive selling policies imposed by providers and hospitals. In fact, several large pharmaceutical companies have laid off more than 30 percent of their sales forces just in the time of this writing.

Despite the challenges of selling in this particular industry, pharmaceutical reps should take comfort in knowing that their products are essential components in every provider's armamentarium. Medications are crucial in treating all diseases. In the field of cardiology for example, much of the success that we have in treating heart disease is due to the many wonderful medications at our disposal. Moreover, without those products many patients would die.

I have had the privilege of interacting with pharmaceutical representatives for the better part of two decades; as a student, trainee and finally as a cardiologist. In that time I have formed very definite impressions about these sales professionals. In general I have found them to be bright, committed, concerned about patients and their customers and generally fun to be around. But I have also found them to be chronically timid by nature. Or at least that is the impression that I get as a result of the deferential and submissive demeanor they consistently seem to demonstrate around providers and staff. I am also of the belief that this apparent demeanor is not an individual or personal preference but instead results from the direct expectations of their superiors in management. It is this problem, in my opinion, that is in large part responsible for the troubles in their industry.

Certainly, pharmaceutical reps have their share of hurdles. Regulations and oversight often dictate what they can say, when then can say it and who they can say it to. But they don't dictate *how* it is said. In sales, the demeanor of the seller is just as important, if not more so, than the message itself. It is absolutely essential to always engage with your customers on an equal footing. Entering a business relationship without mutual respect is suicidal. If you're thinking that's easier said than done, then you need to change your thinking. Because anything less will keep you from fully recognizing your true potential.

Consider Pyrametrics again for the moment. If you recall, the system requires you to first think in terms of the broad and then move to the specific. In thinking about your customers keep in mind that healthcare providers undergo very rigorous training. Much of that training deals with making decisions quickly and then defending them against what can be very harsh criticism.

Because of this most providers are very confident in their abilities. This attitude is absolutely essential in doing their job.

If you think about yourself, you are much more likely to respond favorably to someone who comes to you as an equal, with confidence and integrity, than you would some who does not do these things. The same is true with your customers. Healthcare is a very large and complex industry and it takes many different partners, all working together, to provide quality patient care. One of those partners is you. Your actions make a difference in patient care. First, you need to believe it. Then you need to make your customers believe it too. This is as true for selling pharmaceuticals as it is for anything else.

NON-TECHNOLOGY-RELATED PRODUCTS AND SERVICES

Healthcare consumes a wide range of products and services that are not considered technology-related, although many employ technology to function.

Financial Services & Insurance

Beyond patient billing and collections, medical practices need general financial management, accounting and bookkeeping services. While many of these capabilities are available in practice management systems, some are not. Providers may choose to purchase the appropriate software and systems and handle this in-house; others outsource by contracting with a service provider.

Other financial services include retirement planning, pension plans and investment vehicles. It is a known fact that as reimbursements continue to drop, the healthcare industry as a whole will be looking for new and more creative ways to offset these losses. As the previous sections have eluded to, declining reimbursements are driving many unpopular decisions in healthcare. While this is very unsettling for your customers, it is an opportunity for you.

Another important area is insurance. Medical service providers are like any other company in their need for a wide variety of insurance products. For hospitals and providers malpractice and liability insurance top the list. Other insurance needs include:

- Health, life and specialty coverage as part of the employee benefits package.
- Disability.
- Workers compensation coverage as required by state law.
- Property insurance to protect the facility, equipment, furnishings and other contents.
- Auto insurance if the operation owns vehicles.
- Key employee life and/or disability.
- Business interruption insurance.
- Umbrella policies to protect against losses above the limits of other policies.

Keep in mind, success in sales is a direct byproduct of strong relationships. And strong relationships are formed when your customers believe that you know them, care about them and have their best interests at heart. It is therefore prudent to take your knowledge of the industry and apply it in such a way as to resonate with your customers on a personal level to solve their most pressing problems. When it comes to financial and insurance matters, there are few things more pressing.

Healthcare: A Different Kind of Customer

As an industry, healthcare has a number of unique characteristics when it comes to purchasing. This is why you not only need to know your product thoroughly, you also need to understand the role your product plays in the overall operation of your customers. You need to know *what* else they're buying, *why* they're buying and *how* your product supports the solution that is best for them.

This does *not* mean that a pharmaceutical rep selling chemotherapy treatment needs to know as much as the oncologist about drug action at the cellular level.

It does, however, mean that you must understand how your products relate to the overall treatment process so you can explain why your solution is best, answer questions and leverage successes with one provider type to others when applicable and appropriate.

A substantial portion of the products purchased by the healthcare industry have a direct impact on patient care. Considerably more have an indirect impact. Very little of what these customers buy doesn't in some way effect the patient experience and/or the life and health of individuals. If you're thinking that's a tremendous responsibility for everyone, you are absolutely right. Your ability to demonstrate your understanding of this issue will strengthen your relationship with your customers and give you an edge over your competitors.

Something else to keep in mind, which we will discuss in more detail in Chapter 4, is that the people making the purchases are often not professional buyers. They may be physicians, other provider professionals, medical or non-medical technicians or administrative staffers ranging from a receptionist to an office manager. Even as they want to be in control, they will look to you to guide them through the sales process.

Finally, as an industry, healthcare is heavily regulated and those regulations can impact the purchasing processes. Find out what regulations effect your particular product or service and guide your customers so they maintain compliance at all times.

SCALE AND COMPLEXITY

While most healthcare providers purchase pretty much the same type of things (appropriate to their specialty, of course), the scale and complexity of these purchases will vary widely. A medical clinic may have a dozen exam rooms while a hospital has several hundred beds, multiple intensive care units, an emergency department and other specialty facilities and clinics. Both entities need most of the items we've just discussed, but the volume the hospital consumes is likely to be markedly higher, and the complexity of the sale is likely to be greater as well.

Your pre-call research should include an analysis of the scale and complexity of potential customers. We'll talk more about how to conduct that research in Chapter 7. Your goal is to invest your time and energy developing profitable accounts.

Let's look at this strictly from the sales rep's perspective and keep it simple for illustration purposes. Here's the scenario: Your commission is one percent of the gross dollar amount of your sales. A hospital buys 1,000 units and a small medical practice buys 25. Your basic price is $5 per unit, which is what the medical practice pays. But the hospital is able to qualify for a quantity discount of $2.50 per unit.

So the hospital is going to pay $2,500.00, of which you'll get $25. The medical practice is going to pay $125, and your commission is $1.25. Of course you're going to make more on the hospital, but what you also have to consider is how long it's going to take you to do the work. If the hospital sale takes you 10 hours to complete, great. If it takes you 40 hours to complete, not so much. And it's similar with the medical practice. Is the effort involved in making the sale proportionately smaller or about the same?

Your real life transactions will not be that simple, but the concept is. A basic rule of thumb is that the larger the practice, the greater the opportunities – but those opportunities will likely be more complex and challenging.

At the heart of Pyrametrics is the analytical mindset - knowing why something happens and how you can use that information to your benefit. This applies equally as well to understanding customer behavior as it does to understanding what deals you should be involved with. Now that you understand what is being bought and why, let's take a look at who is doing the buying.

CHAPTER 4

IDENTIFYING THE BUYERS

"Who Dares Wins" - Motto of the British Army's Special Air Service

In B2B sales, the customer is technically a company but the buyer is always a person. You may sell a huge piece of high-tech operating room equipment to a hospital, a software package to a specialty service provider or supplies to a medical practice – it doesn't matter. What matters is that the decision to buy is made by human beings who buy from other human beings, not companies. More important is that they prefer to buy from people they know, like and trust. When you apply Pyrametrics – taking the complex and breaking it down to its simplest parts – not only as a methodology but as a mindset, you'll see its value in this aspect of sales. In the complex matter of relationship building, the process begins by learning about your customers in general. Then taking that information and refining it so that you can truly understand your customers individually.

Knowing your customers, both the companies and the people, is a foundation of Pyrametrics. The buyers within the healthcare industry often have characteristics that are not shared by buyers in other industries. As we've already noted, they tend to be highly-educated and don't always respond well to the sales process or those engaged in it. The industry itself is extremely hierarchical and political. The information in this chapter and the next is designed to help you gain some insight about the people and places you'll be calling on, how they relate to each other, how they are likely to relate to you and how you can use that information to be more successful.

PHYSICIANS

In the healthcare industry, physicians are at the top of the metaphoric food chain. This is not meant to slight anyone else in the business, it's a simple statement of fact because (at least as of this writing) physicians are ultimately responsible for the patients, so they call the shots.

Your understanding of physicians begins with the knowledge that the process of becoming a physician is lengthy, rigorous and competitive. Competition begins in high school and continues all the way up the ladder. That is why doctors tend to be highly motivated, self directed and goal oriented and yes, occasionally arrogant and egotistical. They are ultimately responsible for patient care in an environment where responsibilities and workload are rising at the same time reimbursements are dropping across the board, and where mergers and acquisitions contribute to a constantly changing landscape.

There are two types of physicians that practice medicine in the United States: those who hold the Doctor of Medicine (MD) degree and those who hold the Doctor of Osteopathic Medicine (DO) degree. Both types of physicians are well trained, competent and can practice equally in the United States. The primary difference is that, in addition to the standard medical curriculum, osteopathic medical students receive additional training in the art of manipulative medicine. In today's practice environment, there is very little distinction between MDs and DOs, and you will likely encounter both types of physicians throughout your career.

Training to become a physician can take up to a decade or longer depending on what path is chosen. Education begins after college with four years of medical school. It is from there that a career selection is made. That selection begins with the residency program. Depending on what field is chosen, residency can last three to seven years. Following residency, some physicians continue on for further training. That process is called fellowship and it is the path to becoming a specialist. Like residency, fellowships vary depending on the discipline; traditionally, one to four more years. In my experience, after graduating from medical school I completed three years of residency in internal medicine and then had to complete a three year fellowship in cardiology in order to treat heart patients.

As alluded to above, physicians are generally classified as either primary care (generalists) or specialists.

PRIMARY CARE INCLUDE	SPECIALTIES INCLUDE
Family Practice	Allergy and Immunology
Internal Medicine	Cardiology
Pediatrics; and sometimes	Critical Care
Obstetrics and Gynecology (OB-GYN)	Dermatology
	Emergency Medicine
	Endocrinology
	Gastroenterology
	Hematology
	Nephrology
	Neurology
	Ophthalmology
	Oncology
	Pathology
	Physical Medicine & Rehabilitation (Physiatry)
	Psychiatry
	Pulmonology
	Radiology
	Radiation Oncology
	Surgery (All types)

Within the specialty ranks, some physicians continue on with additional training to focus on one very specific area. They are considered sub-specialists. An example of a subspecialist is an electrophysiologist, which is a cardiologist who works specifically with heart rhythm problems. Other examples include orthopedic or sports medicine physicians that work on just shoulders or knees, or hepatologists who are gastroenterologists that deal exclusively with the liver and transplant surgeons.

Appendix explains the various specialties in greater detail and will be a good reference for you. Make sure that you always take the time to know who you're calling on and what they actually do as few things are more infuriating to physicians than being approached by a rep who hasn't taken the time to prepare adequately. I don't know how many times I had this conversation:

"Hi Dr. Moronell. I was wondering if you would like to try our newest drug?"

"Thanks, but I don't treat that particular disease."

"But I thought you're a cardiologist, aren't you?"

"Yes, I'm a cardiologist. But I'm not *that kind* of cardiologist."

"I beg your pardon."

"You know, there are at least four different cardiology types: non-invasive, invasive/non-interventional, interventional and electrophysiology. I'm the second one. You need to speak with..."

Situations like this are uncomfortable for everyone. I didn't like being snippy but neither did I appreciate having my time wasted; no physician would. Therefore, before you make your first call, study the doctor's bio, speak with the nurses or the staff and do whatever additional research is necessary to understand the focus and scope of the practice. You'll be glad you did.

You'll also find that various specialties attract unique personality types. There are no universal distinctions, but enough commonalities exist to make a few generalizations. Surgeons, by and large, are hard-driving, type A personalities. So are many cardiologists and those who deal with acute, life threatening situations. By virtue of their workplace demands and responsibilities, they often don't have time to really mull something over. They're used to making decisions quickly and moving on. Consequently, their dealings with sales people may be abrupt as well.

While there are many providers that would be amenable to longer, more in depth conversations, no one is going to respond favorably to a rep who is not well prepared. And because all physicians are under a lot of pressure, you may get barked at even when you really did do everything right. Therefore, if you're a wilting violet or someone whose feelings are easily hurt, perhaps a different occupation is in order.

It's also convenient and generally accurate to characterize physicians as either patient-focused or procedure-focused. This is valuable to know when qualifying leads and figuring out how to best spend your time. This is not to suggest that some physicians are not interested in patients, because everyone is. This simply points out that some specialists are more involved with procedures than others. Physicians who enjoy more involved, long term traditional relationships with patients may consider one route (those offering less procedures include family practice, psychiatry, pediatrics, internal medicine), where those who enjoy more hands on, tactile processes with potentially shorter term patient relationships and more immediate gratification may choose another (surgery, cardiology, gastroenterology, radiology, emergency medicine, ophthalmology, radiation oncology, critical care). The characteristics these physicians demonstrate in their practice choices can carry over into their relationships with colleagues, subordinates and salespeople. This kind of information is very important to know because it will help give you insight into how you should engage and deal with these customers.

As a general rule, physicians tend to be very independent, often resisting anyone they think is looking to drive their behavior or change their minds – which is what you, as a sales professional, are trying to do. Of course, that's a good thing if the decision is in your favor – not so good if it isn't. That's why your goal is to become an advisor they trust and are comfortable turning to for guidance, information and solutions.

A Very Exclusive Club

The number one reason clients call me is for help getting in front of physicians and other providers. It's true, one of the biggest hurdles reps must overcome is trying to get face time. It's important to remember that physicians are people too. And people tend to be more receptive to those they have things in common with. When I was in practice there were a handful of partners that I argued with on a near daily basis. In fact, there were times when I was so angry with them that I was glad to be a cardiologist - it was the only reason I was able to ward off having a heart attack. And I'm sure they were equally frustrated with me. That was just part of life in a big group. But regardless of how angry we may have been, we would always defer to each other over an outsider. Unfortunately, it's not uncommon for sales people to be considered outsiders by their physician customers.

The reason for this bias is undoubtedly a result of the training that we all shared. Medical school is challenging but it's nothing like residency and fellowship where the physical and emotional demands can really take their toll. It's something that folks outside the profession can't really relate to unless they've been through it. You hear this kind of thing from soldiers all the time. And while I'm certainly not trying to equate medicine with combat, physician training is still tough.

I recall some months during residency where I worked over 120 hours a week. It was absolutely brutal; physically and emotionally. I recall times being so tired that it was almost laughable. One night I fixed a chilidog for dinner (I wasn't a cardiologist then). The last thing I remember is laying on the floor to watch television. The next morning I awoke with the chilidog stuck to my face. It seems I passed out before even taking a bite. A friend of mine told me he fell asleep in the shower and got wedged in the stall. The point is that every physician has gone through this in one way or another. And they know their colleagues have too. It's as though they've created an exclusive club with very stringent membership criteria.

So, as you work to engage your physician customers, keep in mind that while you may not always be successful on the first try that doesn't mean you still can't earn their respect. You can. It will just take time, persistence and an unwavering commitment to them and their patients.

Doctors and Burnout

Job burnout hits physicians more often than most other employed people in the U.S. In a study of more than 7,000 doctors, nearly half reported at least one symptom of burnout, including emotional exhaustion, a high degree of cynicism or depersonalization toward their patients. Burned-out doctors are more prone to thinking about suicide and making medical errors than their peers. The burn-out rate was highest among doctors at the "frontline of care," such as family, emergency and internal medicine. Researchers weren't clear on why burnout strikes so many doctors, but likely reasons include excessive workloads, too much paperwork, loss of professional autonomy and higher patient loads to make up for declining reimbursement rates.

Another survey, commissioned by The Physicians Foundation, revealed that 60 percent of practicing doctors would retire today if given the opportunity. Discontent and frustration is running high among physicians, and those emotions are reflected in how they function with patients and in the general management of their practices. Remember to use this kind of general information as a primer before engaging with specific customers. Having a strong base of knowledge helps you build deeper and more lasting relationships with your customers.

OTHER HEALTHCARE PROVIDERS

As part of selling to the healthcare industry, you're likely to encounter a wide range of practitioners and staff that are part of the care delivery team. These professionals are essential to the mission of their organizations and often are either decision-makers or strong decision-influencers when it comes to purchasing. It's important to understand the relationship each of these professionals has within their respective organizations so you can craft messages that are relevant to them. Physicians often give heavy weight to the recommendations of their staff when making a buying decision, so you should consider these decision-influences as you develop and implement your sales strategy. Don't take a one-size-fits-all approach – every organization will be different in ways that range from subtle to dramatic.

Mid-Level Providers

Mid-level providers include nurse practitioners, nurse anesthetists and physician assistants who extend the physician's capabilities by treating patients with routine, less-complicated issues and procedures. In many cases, mid-level providers function with high autonomy and may even be fully licensed and autonomous providers, sometimes with their own practices. Where mid-level providers operate independently in their own practices, they are the decision-makers and have ultimate buying authority. In other settings, they may or may not be the final decision-maker (depending on the product), but are often decision-influencers.

Nurses

Nurses play a critical, multifaceted role on the healthcare team. In the hospital, nurses provide care at every stage of a patient's stay. They can also hold middle- and upper-management positions and may be responsible for policy and purchasing decisions on a variety of goods and services within their specific areas. In most larger hospitals, there is a chief nursing officer (CNO) responsible for overseeing the entire nursing staff. Some hospital CEOs come from the nursing ranks. In medical practices, nurses are the primary interface between the physician and the patients, and are usually responsible for prescription refills, first-line patient inquiries and even certain process and management decisions.

Technologists

Technologists are specifically-trained individuals who assist with various kinds of testing and procedures, such as imaging (X-ray, MRI, echocardiography, ultrasound, and so on) or specific procedures (cardiac catheterization, surgery, anesthesia, radiology, and so on). Technologists rarely have final purchase authority but are often very influential when it comes to purchasing decisions on equipment and supplies they use.

WHERE TO START - APPROACHING THE MEDICAL ACCOUNT

You have just been handed a lead about an opportunity with a medical practice in your territory. As part of the Pyrametrics Process you know that learning as much as you can about your customer prior to making the first call is critical for sales success. With that in mind, what are the key questions that you'll need to answer immediately?

A. Practice type - What is their specialty?

This question deals exclusively with identifying and understanding the specialty type of your physician customers. Depending on what you sell, this is critical information. Pharmaceutical representatives, for example, will target their specific customers by the diseases their medications are designed to treat. If you are going to sell eye drops to treat glaucoma, for example, you will not be interested in an orthopedic surgery practice. They are also interested in the size and locations of the practice, where the providers generally work (hospitals, offices, imaging centers, etc.) and the rules of engagement within the account.

Health Information Technology (HIT) and telecommunications personnel will be more interested in the infrastructure of the practice and the degree of complexity of the organization rather than what types of diseases are being treated. "Complexity" refers to the number of offices, number of providers, distances traveled between hospital and offices, dependency on technology, imaging needs, security and redundancy needs, disaster recovery, overall use of technology for practice operations, cost containment and demonstrating ROI.

Biotechnology (or device) vendors will likely deal with surgical or medical specialists in a hospital or outpatient surgery center type environment. Specialized equipment manufacturers will likely work in the hospital setting while insurance or financial services personnel will spend the bulk of their time in providers' offices.

The type of specialist can also indicate their imaging requirements. Having a large imaging capability often indicates a larger practice with bigger budgets and more complex needs. This can be an important distinction when deciding of how best to spend your time.

Be aware that many practices have very strict rules about how sales people can interact with the business. Take the time to learn these rules upfront so you can insure that each of your visits conforms to their specific standards. Nothing will damage your reputation faster than to be seen as not complying with the rules of engagement.

B. Number of providers. How many potential customers can be found under one roof?

Pyrametrics extols the virtues of efficiency. If you are going to make a call at a customer site, it is beneficial to know how many customers may be there, what they do, what their basic needs appear to be and how receptive they will be to speaking with you. The number of providers is critically important for technology vendors such as EMR companies, for example, because the more providers there are the more data and images will need to managed and disseminated. There will also be increased needs for security, redundancy and back up as well.

C. Coverage area. Where are your customers seeing their patients and doing their procedures?

This information is very important because many times, in order to speak with your customers, you'll need to be where they are. If they spend time at the hospital, then you need to be there also. If they have offices in three different counties, you'll need to be there too. The number of locations also increases the complexity of their organization (see above). Depending on what you are selling, this could be very critical for your business.

D. Status of the practice. Is your customer part of an independent group or an employee of a practice that is owned by a hospital?

This information is very important, especially nowadays. With the current healthcare climate, many practices are aligning with, partnering with or selling out completely to hospitals. In the latter case, physicians that work for hospitals now no longer may be in a position to make local purchasing decisions. Before wasting your time selling to someone who cannot buy always make sure your contacts have the proper authority to make things happen.

E. Governance. What is the management structure?

If the practice is still independent, try and ascertain the form of governance they use. In many smaller practices for example, physicians can make decisions quickly and efficiently. One doctor equals one boss. The larger the group however, the more complex and difficult it may be for anyone to make a decision. Understanding governance issues is commonplace when calling on healthcare providers and something that you will simply have to learn to adjust to up front.

Physicians by nature, can very inexperienced when it comes to business decisions. They are also quite conservative, by and large. In most groups, although there may be a governing body (executive committee, board of directors, managing partners), all the physicians are likely owners and/or partners too. Therefore, all may have a say in the purchasing process even if they're not listed as part of the management team. So just because one physician may tell you the buy is a "go" doesn't mean that it truly is.

Consider a medical group as like a ship with many captains. In order to be successful selling to most medical groups you need to learn the personalities of, and as much about, as many of the captains that you can. This may not be an easy process but it is really the only way to approach a medical group and is why doing your homework is so important for your success.

Knowing how to characterize your opportunities by understanding that all physicians are not created equal, do not practice equally or need the same goods and services is an important first step in the Pyrametrics process - understanding your customers. The information presented herein will set you on a proper course to making that happen. In the next chapter we move on to another very important customer type, the hospital system.

CHAPTER 5

MORE ABOUT THE BUYERS

"A hospital, what is it? It's a big building with patients but that's not important right now." - From the motion picture, Airplane!

Contrary to the above quotation, hospitals are very important right now. In fact, if you are in healthcare sales, they very well may represent your biggest opportunities. It is essential you develop a good working knowledge of how they're managed, how they operate and who the key decision makers are.

Hospitals come in many shapes and sizes with varying missions and responsibilities. Also, depending on what you're selling, it may be necessary to move beyond the familiar customer type and call on folks you've never met before or are not familiar with. Consider health information technology for example, nowadays you can't discuss any aspect of hospital operations without also considering the HIT ramifications. Consequently, it may not be sufficient to just call on the CIO or CTO, instead you'll need to *sell through* the entire organization and call on people who previously may have only been on the periphery of your radar screen.

Therefore, instead of trying to explain every possible encounter, I believe that you will be better served by learning how to learn about them on your own. And in that regard Pyrametrics is a very powerful tool because the skills introduced in this chapter will enable you to do just that and to build a base of knowledge, applicable anywhere, that can then be individualized to meet your specific sales situations.

THE HOSPITAL SYSTEM

In chapter 2 you were introduced to the various hospital types in the industry. Calling on hospitals is considerably different from calling on providers in an independent medical group as there is a definite hierarchy with key personnel having very defined roles and responsibilities. There are also very well established protocols, rules of engagement and purchasing patterns which you'll need to learn. Where a medical practice can be all over the map structurally, most hospitals are organized in a similar way and probably very much like the company you work for.

When I was practicing medicine, we used to have a partners' meeting every Monday morning. Despite our best efforts, those meetings always degraded into a "free for all" where information would be debated down to the subatomic level rendering any decision making nearly impossible. In the rare instance that a decision was made, it was almost certainly rehashed (and overturned) the following week by guys who'd missed the previous meeting. So dysfunctional were the meetings, that over time many partners quit coming. In the end we gave up on the Monday meeting as a decision making venue.

One day I had the opportunity to attend a meeting hosted by the hospital CEO that was attended by many of his executive team. I recall being struck by the professionalism and the organized manner in which decisions were made. The CEO would lead off with a topic, a brief discussion would follow and then there would be a vote. And, just like that, a decision was made. It was a beautiful thing to behold. As you call on more and more customers, it is always wise to learn how their decisions are made and be prepared to adapt to whatever system is used. Also, try not to get frustrated if your customer's decision making process takes a while. You never know what issues they're facing. So you have to be patient.

As you approach the hospitals, remember Pyrametrics and the need to first build a general knowledge base. This is as vital here as it was in dealing with groups. Remember that even though hospitals can be big, complex and difficult to manage, everything is easier when broken down into its simplest parts. When it comes to understanding hospitals, there are three issues that are critical whether you're selling in San Francisco, Ft. Lauderdale or any spot in between. Once you've nailed this, you can study the ramifications to your local markets and at your individual customer sites.

THE THREE MOST CRITICAL ISSUES TO HOSPITALS

1. Attracting and retaining quality providers into their networks.

Hospitals and providers function in a symbiotic relationship. Providers need places to treat their patients that offer the most appealing, cost effective and technologically relevant equipment and services available. Hospitals need providers to bring in patients and fill their rooms, operating suites, intensive care units, imaging centers and emergency departments. Hospitals would not exist without providers and providers could do very little for their patients without hospitals. Despite this obvious co-dependence, relationships between providers and hospitals are rarely idyllic. The reality is that although hospitals and providers depend on each other, many times they are fiercely competing against each other as well. Consider the following example.

The market for cardiology services in a medium sized market in the northwest is dominated by one large, independent cardiology group and two competing hospital systems. The group has wisely maintained their independence and sought to support both hospitals equally versus aligning exclusively with one over the other. As cardiology services are quite lucrative each hospital has reacted to this posture by extending themselves greatly in an attempt to win the favor of the sole cardiology group.

While both the hospitals and group function symbiotically in the treatment of cardiac patients, they compete aggressively as well. Both the group and hospitals vie for the highly reimbursable imaging opportunities essential to each business. Hospital A, the larger of the two, allowed the cardiology group to place their own catheterization lab and imaging center on leased space despite the obvious revenue losses that this would create. They did this because they realized (correctly) that fostering better relations with the group, even at the risk of short-term revenue loss, would only improve their position over time. This was a substantial win for Hospital A over their competitor.

When the cardiology group was looking to upgrade offices, both hospitals offered optimal spaces at very attractive rates. When the group was looking to hire on more cardiologists, both hospitals aided in their recruiting efforts. Both hospitals also attempt to entice the group to refer patients by offering convenient data sharing opportunities, lucrative management contracts and opportunities for joint ventures. And both hospitals continue to demonstrate their willingness to align and engage even deeper with the cardiology group.

Only time will tell which hospital, if either, will win the total allegiance of the group. But for the winner, the rewards will likely be substantial. Certainly that is why they are pulling out all the stops now.

The above case illustrates the lengths that hospitals are willing to go to foster good relations with their provider colleagues even if some of the initiatives result in short term revenue losses. This interrelationship is very important for you as a new sales professionals to understand because these types of arrangements are happening all over the country. It is likely that your customers will be talking about these types of arrangements too. Armed with this information, you can now begin to craft messages that place your products and services in a relevant context. And also by doing so you are demonstrating to the customer your grasp on their key issues.

2. Competing and winning in ever-increasingly competitive markets.

While some hospitals may operate in small, independent and isolated markets, most do not. In fact it would be rare, if not impossible, to find a hospital that is not concerned about a competitor somewhere. Therefore, consider any medium to large city in the United States. Not only is there likely to be more than one hospital in that particular market, it is an absolute certainty that they are in competition with each other.

Hospitals depend on patients for their survival and as a result, everything they do is in an attempt to retain the ones they have and obtain new ones. Hospitals obtain patients in three principle ways:

A. Through direct referrals from providers. As discussed above, hospitals depend on the providers within their *networks* to bring patients in the door.

B. As mandated by the patient's specific payer. Many insurance companies have relationships with hospitals to treat their patients. Therefore, when a patient carrying a certain insurance type needs care they know to go that specific hospital. These relationships with insurance companies are very important for the hospitals and they compete fiercely for each contract. However, they are not easily obtained because the insurance companies are demanding a serious ROI for their commitments. In order to win these contracts hospitals have to demonstrate some advantage over their competition. This advantage could be on cost of care, patient satisfaction, key service line availability, specialized provider access or any combination of the above. Hospitals therefore are continuously looking to become more efficient, keep costs down, entice the best providers, offer the newest services and generate the best outcomes.

C. Through independent patient selection. Many patients have the luxury of not being required to use one hospital exclusively. Medicare patients, for example, often can seek care at various hospitals. For patients like these hospitals compete for their business through DTC (direct to the consumer) activities such as television commercials, radio spots, open houses, social media, community activities and specific disease-awareness programs like breast and prostate cancer.

3. Maintaining fiscal viability despite markedly declining compensation.

This topic has been discussed previously but is still bears repeating. Hospitals are being asked to care for sicker, more complicated patients despite a climate of declining reimbursement. Every hospital function must contribute favorably to the bottom line. The pressure to optimize performance reaches every department in the building.

As a sales professional, you need to continually keep these points in perspective as you position your products and services. If you can demonstrate that what you sell will help give the hospital a leg up on their competition, they will be more inclined to listen to you. Furthermore, as you compete for the attention of your customers, make sure to always communicate in such a way that is interesting and relevant. If you haven't picked up on it already, the overriding theme of this book is preparation. This is the most important part of the sales cycle and the time when you must execute well.

IDENTIFYING THE KEY PLAYERS

Hospitals are likely to be structured more along the lines of a traditional corporation and employ the same titles found in other industries (such as CEO, COO, CFO and so on). They will also have a sophisticated purchasing department that could be the primary focal point for all sales contact. Whether you will need to go beyond the purchasing agent or manager depends on what you're selling. HIT suppliers, for example, need to work with the CIO or CTO in addition to or sometimes instead of the purchasing department. Pharmaceutical sales people may engage exclusively with clinical types while financial services reps work with the CFO.

Though the operational structure of a hospital might resemble that of any business of a similar size, physicians will likely be involved in purchases that directly and indirectly effect patient care, from actual imaging and treatment equipment to information products to products and services related to quality and cost control.

Surprisingly, you may find physicians involved in the purchase of nonmedical items such as furnishings and aesthetically related things. Remember, physician recruitment and retention are high priorities for hospitals. When physicians find a hospital warm, inviting and tastefully decorated, they may be more inclined to refer patients to that facility. Similarly, if patients or their families complain about a hospital's ambiance, physicians may be reluctant to send other patients there.

When I was practicing, a regional hospital I frequented spent literally millions of dollars on remodeling and redecorating its main lobby. The result was beautiful. But the ICU hadn't been updated in at least two decades. It not only looked outdated, it wasn't as functional as it should have been. There was an awkwardly positioned counter that one of my former partners would repeatedly bump into; he used to complain that he'd had the same bruise for 25 years. When we and other physicians saw that the hospital was willing to invest in the facility, we complained about the ICU. The hospital listened and asked for our input on the upgrades.

Another example involved a local hospital's relationship with a prominent cardiovascular surgeon. The surgeon was looking to develop a better relationship with a community hospital to the north. In response, the local hospital worked with the surgeon on an ambitious telemedicine program to boost referrals. These types of dedicated partnerships were not uncommon.

The key point you need to remember is to never assume you know who the decision-makers and decision-influencers are. Always find out for sure and then regularly reconfirm, because healthcare environments are fluid, alliances come and go and unique partnerships occur all the time.

Where To Start - Approaching the Hospital

This section highlights many of the key players and industry-relevant topics that you will need to address during your tenure as a hospital sales professional. Also included are some basic questions that will get you thinking about the best ways to craft your specific messages.

As you begin to develop your sales strategy, keep Pyrametrics in mind as you work from the general to the specific and the complex to the simple. Realize that there are many different people to contact and many important discussions to have. Always strive to be organized and methodical in your preparation and execution. You'll find that while it may take a little longer, you'll be much more likely to broaden your reach and avoid missing anything. Furthermore, as you move deliberately through the account you'll begin to find that your reputation precedes you. As your accolades grow, so too will your confidence. Once this happens, success isn't far behind.

One possible approach for calling on hospitals is presented below.

I. Identify the key personnel within the organization.

Hospitals are organized very much like most other corporations. In addition to the purchasing department that you should know very well, some of the other folks you may be calling on are outlined on the following pages. When it comes to meeting new customers that you may not have been exposed to before, remember to always keep Pyrametrics in mind and plan accordingly. Developing, maintaining and executing a detailed and comprehensive plan will help you succeed where other, less prepared reps fail.

CEO/ADMINISTRATOR		
Strategic/tactical focus	**Key Issues**	**Opportunities**
Global (institutional level) project identification and execution. Relationship building. Overall institutional management.	Revenue management. Physician retention. Competition. Market share Growth (New market development, enhanced referrals) and Retention. Increased service line offerings. Evolving care-delivery models.	Differentiate your company at the highest level. Get "specked in" at project outset. Reduce competitive effectivity. Get top-down referral power. Trusted advisorship status quickly.

COO (CHIEF OPERATING OFFICER)		
Strategic/tactical focus	**Key Issues**	**Opportunities**
Departmental level project identification and execution. General management.	Implementing strategic plans. Tactical initiatives. Finding and developing functional efficiencies. Institutional cost reduction and ROI.	Can get specific program information, timelines, budgeting, etc. They can facilitate communications with underlings.

CMO (CHIEF MEDICAL OFFICER/MEDICAL DIRECTOR)		
Strategic/tactical focus	**Key Issues**	**Opportunities**
This may be a difficult meeting to arrange. Probe for provider-specific issues related to your technology.	They deal primarily with providers and medical issues pertaining to patient care. Information technology is frequently an issue. Quality is frequently an issue. Pharmaceutical issues may be addressed also.	Can get a physician perspective on the issues within the group relevant to your product or service line. Could be a strong ally if a relationship is developed.

PHYSICIAN LIAISON/ADMINISTRATIVE SUPPORT PERSON		
Strategic/tactical focus	**Key Issues**	**Opportunities**
This person is tasked with identifying provider issues and solving them from an overall hospital basis. He/she is the hospital sales person for maintaining relationships with providers. They are your counterparts in the hospital setting.	Unhappy providers - you can probe to find out if they are unhappy due to things that you can impact. Referral network maintenance and expansion.	They know EVERY provider, organizational leader and key player. You can test your ideas out on this person first. Can potentially leverage referrals to other places. Probe for areas of provider pain relative to your service line.

CNO (CHIEF NURSING OFFICER)/CLINICAL MANAGER

Strategic/tactical focus	**Key Issues**	**Opportunities**
Responsible for all nursing and support related issues.	They deal with all the nursing-related issues. Nurses use the medications and technology significantly. Nurses are VERY aware of hospital issues and can be influential.	Can obtain pain point information. Can leverage new referrals. Can be POC or advisor to you.

CTO/CIO (CHIEF TECHNOLOGY/INFORMATION OFFICER)

Strategic/tactical focus	**Key Issues**	**Opportunities**
This is the technology leader. Probe for strategic and tactical level projects. EMR, internal and external connectivity links. Security Redundancy Accessibility Connect with satellite clinics Hardware, software and peripherals	They must implement all new tech initiatives. Maintain all tech products/services. Be aware of emerging technologies and ideas. They are reviewed based on how well they do 1, 2, 3 above.	Speck in your products at ground level. Have a direct "in" with key technology decision-maker. Can establish unique relationship - you can both advise and help each other to meet your individual goals. Understand the entire inner workings of the IT/telecommunications dept.

IMAGING CENTER MANAGER		
Strategic/tactical focus	**Key Issues**	**Opportunities**
They are responsible for much of the revenue in a hospital setting.	Maintaining data transfer capabilities and core imaging services.	There is NOTHING more important than getting their data from place to place securely, timely, accurately and dependably.

FACILITIES MANAGER		
Strategic/tactical focus	**Key Issues**	**Opportunities**
They keep the place running.	Maintaining the facilities from an operational and maintenance standpoint.	They can give you a layout of all the technology as well as problems and opportunities.

LEAD/MANAGING PHARMACIST		
Strategic/tactical focus	**Key Issues**	**Opportunities**
Oversee the usage and acquisition of medication on the hospital formulary.	Maintaining an adequate formulary of medications. Meeting provider demand. Following cost containment strategies.	Essential for pharmaceutical representatives to deal with.

II. Make certain to have a plan. Having a playbook helps you stay organized. Many hospitals are large and complex and there are lots of different people, all with various roles and responsibilities, that you need to manage. In some cases your CRM will help you keep track of contacts and provide for more accurate forecasting, but it won't lay out a call strategy. That is your job. We'll review this concept more in later chapters. But for now train yourself to always think analytically - set a goal, identify the steps, lay out a plan then execute. And never forget to continually reassess, readjust and realign to stay on target.

III. Be deliberate and methodical in your discussions.

In much the same way that an attorney prepares his questions for each witness, the same thing applies in healthcare sales. As you begin to call on these accounts remember that the sales process is just that, a process. It is comprised of a series of important steps that must be done correctly, and in order. Therefore, before you start scheduling appointments, make sure you know what you want to talk about, where you're going with the conversation and what happens next. Have an objective for each and every encounter.

When it comes to understanding hospital operations, there are four areas you need to consider - environmental, organizational, technological and patient care. (Note - the term *technology* is used generically below. Consider your products as the *technology* when reviewing this information.)

1. Environment Specific

The following topics deal with those things contributing to the overall healthcare environment in which hospitals participate.

Reimbursements: Reimbursement is a very important issue facing hospitals in all healthcare markets today. It is important to know that in most hospitals not every department is a money-maker. Many of the more lucrative departments such as radiology, cardiology, surgery and gastroenterology help support the cost of other departments. But because hospitals have to offer a full range of services, they are constantly looking for the most efficients means of providing care available. You need to be sensitive of these requirements and understand how your products will fit into the overall mix.

Sample questions:

- How is the current climate affecting your reimbursements?
- How do you see the effects of the Affordable Care Act (ObamaCare) on your business?
- Are you making any changes in your business operations as a result of reimbursement cuts?
- Would you be willing to discuss (particular issues about your products) if they could help with reimbursements?
- What are the biggest causes of your declining reimbursements?

Competition: As pointed out previously, competition is intense in the healthcare marketplace. Hospitals are continuously looking to foster better relations with there provider communities so that they can obtain greater patient referrals, more lucrative third-party payer contracts and increase their market share.

Always remember to frame your questions and pitch your solutions in such a manner as to demonstrate your understanding of these issues. Your customers will consider you infinitely more valuable if you can demonstrate to them why buying from you will improve their competitive position.

Sample questions:

- Who are your main competitors?
- Are you concerned about your competitive situation?
- Is your technology infrastructure in pace with your competition?
- Can you envision technology helping you win against your competition?
- What about your competition concerns you the most?

Market share: Just as sales are a byproduct of strong relationships, market share for hospitals is a byproduct of a strong referral network, effective patient care and efficient operations. As a solution provider, you can enhance your customer's market share by first understanding their needs and then crafting solutions that help them serve their patients better. Remember always, what you sell can directly impact your customer's position. Make certain to always do your best.

Sample questions:

- Are you satisfied with your current market share?
- Do you see technology affecting your market share?
- What types of technology could help you with market share?
- Is your lack of technology limiting your increasing market share?
- Is a market share advantage worth the cost of technology to your business?

Governmental effects: Healthcare operations are significantly influenced by the actions of federal, state and local governments. And although you personally have little influence on those entities, your industry may be more engaged. As a sales professional you still need to keep abreast of the latest policy changes as they will most certainly have an effect on your customers. Also, framing your message in the context of current policies demonstrates your grasp on the market and leads you closer to trusted advisorship.

Sample questions:

- How are HIPAA & HITECH affecting your business?
- Would a technology buy improve your compliance?
- Are government regulations/new laws effecting your ability to offer your service?
- Are you looking at specific purchases within the next 3-6 months to address these government mandates?
- Are you prepared to meet meaningful use requirements?

2. Organization Specific

The following topics deal with organizational factors specific to each hospital.

Hospital Type: Several different types of hospitals exist. They are:

A. General (Community) - The most common type of facility established to acquire and treat patients with common diseases.

B. District (tertiary) - The major healthcare center serving a particular area. Because of their higher level of care capabilities (intensive care, child birth, trauma, etc.) they often receive patients in transfer from other institutions.

C. Specialized - Hospitals established to care for unique or certain particular patient types (trauma center, psychiatric, children's, geriatric, etc.)

D. Academic - Hospitals affiliated with colleges or universities and whose major function is to provide education to providers in training.

E. Government - Hospitals that serve a unique patient demographic (Military/VA, Indian Health, etc.).

It is important to be familiar with the different type of hospitals as you may be calling on some or all of them. Knowing the specifics about purchasing, administration, buying cycles, patient types, etc., will be very beneficial as you move forward.

Number of hospitals: Many hospitals that you deal with will be a part of larger institutions or systems. These systems may encompass many different facilities in many different markets. Whether or not you will have the opportunity to call on all them is a matter for your sales manager. Remember that dealing with more than one hospital offers both opportunities and challenges. Opportunities exist because success in one facility maybe leveraged to others with the network. Challenges occur because any time numbers increase, so too does the difficulty in meeting needs and moving the sales process forward.

Always be logical and deliberate in your dealings with hospital systems. Work first at a smaller level building name recognition and racking up successes. Then, as you do advance, do so in a thoughtful manner that leaves nothing to chance and covers all your bases.

Sample questions:

- How many hospitals in your system?
- Where are they?
- Are services identical?
- What are their specialties?
- Where are purchases made?
- How is technology purchased?

HQ location: Knowing where the headquarters is can be very valuable in dealing with hospitals, particularly if their decision making process requires senior level agreement. It is not unusual for hospitals to be able to purchase locally if the items are small. However larger decisions may need to be made elsewhere. As you advance in the sales process, always make certain you know who has purchasing authority, where that person is located and what protocols govern their buying behavior.

Sample questions:

- Who is responsible for buying your products and services?
- Where is it done?
- Is there standardization throughout your system?
- Can we visit with your leadership?
- Would knowing about success we've made with your other locations be valuable to you here?
- What dollar-level can be signed off on locally?

Service line specifics: Patients are cared for in hospitals. But not all hospitals care for similar patients nor offer the same services. Understanding the specifics about each hospital will enable you to penetrate even deeper within that account and help you uncover opportunities that may have been overlooked previously.

Sample questions:

- What is your catch-man area?
- What are your service lines?
- What is your payer-mix like?
- What technology play a role in managing your service area?
- What technological improvements would enable you to better maintain your service area?

Referrals: Understanding the extent of a hospital's referral network is key for leveraging your products and services across multiple lines. In many cases what you sell to a hospital will be relevant to the providers also. By taking the time to research this particular part about your hospital you may be opening the door even wider to your products and services too.

Sample questions:

- Where do your patients come from?
- Who are your top referral sources?
- Do you use technology to manage your referral sources?
- Who manages your referral network?
- What types of data/information is shared between you and your referral network?

3. Technology Specific - An Overview

As mentioned previously, health information technology has become so ingrained in healthcare that it is now almost impossible to separate out technology discussions from the operational discussions of any hospital or medical group. Knowing how HIT plays a role in any hospital is a valuable skill for every technical sales professional.

Competitive situation: If you are selling HIT it is vital for you to position your products and services relevant to the customer's needs. In almost every case, hospitals will be looking to use HIT to gain an edge over their competitors.

Sample questions:

- Does HIT help your competitive situation?
- Can HIT help you with a specific initiative?
- Is your HIT infrastructure limiting your ability to compete?
- With X, could you achieve Y?
- Are you willing to spend on HIT to improve your competitive situation?

Strategic & Tactical Plans: Hospitals are large businesses and as such many of the projects they are performing today were conceived of many years before and incorporated into their operational plans. Therefore, your sales cycle may be quite long for the products and services you offer. Always be mindful of present opportunities but never lose sight of the future. Consistently work to get your products and services incorporated into your customer's future plans.

Sample questions:

- Do you have a strategic plan for technology?
- Do you have tactical technology plans?
- How far into the future do you plan for technology buys?
- Can you share your plans with me?
- If we could potentially save you money on your current/future technology buys, would you be willing to discuss your plans?

4. Technology Specific - Data Sources & Information Management

Hospitals move a lot of data and in the current healthcare market those needs will only increase. Technical sales professionals need to understand the ramifications of this need and be prepared to address it. As your sales process begins with your research, make certain you understand the specifics of where the data comes from.

Electronic Medical Records (EMR): EMRs can be regarded as a blessing or a curse for your healthcare customers. Regardless of their reputation however, one thing about EMRs is indisputable - they permeate almost every part of the hospital. Make certain that you dig deep and understand as much as possible about this ever-growing segment.

Sample questions:

- What EMR do you use or are you planning to use?
- What stage of adoption are you in?
- What problems/successes are you having?
- What types of data dump into your EMR?
- Is your technology infrastructure sufficient for your current and future EMR needs?

Imaging: The first step in treating disease is making the diagnosis. In many cases that diagnosis is only made through the use of imaging modalities. In today's healthcare market the use of imaging is on the rise and so is the need to get those images from place to place quickly, efficiently and cost-effectively. Because your customers will be looking to you for this capability, you need to understand all about this evolving opportunity.

Sample questions:

- Where are your imaging services performed?
- What services do you provide?
- To whom is the data shared?
- Are you satisfied with your data sharing capabilities?
- Is your referring network satisfied?
- Do you have stand-alone imaging centers?
- Are imaging reimbursement reductions affecting your business?

Communication Specific: When discussing image and data management, remember that the network is only good if customers can obtain the information. Make certain that you understand the specifics of the network; what data is being share, where is it going and who wants to see it? Helping your customer optimize their own network will move you closer toward trusted advisorship.

Sample questions:

- Who do you share data with?
- Who shares data with you?
- Who would you like to be sharing with?
- What problems are you having sharing data?

Implementation Specific: Networks are complex and unique to the hospitals using them. It is likely that many different vendors will have a hand in their development and maintenance. Make certain that you understand who the key players are your customer's network so that you can assist when needed but also replace with your own components if the opportunity arises. Opportunities arise though knowledge and understanding. And both of those start with asking relevant questions.

Sample questions:

- Do you work with other vendors?
- What vendors partners do you work with?
- Do you work with specific vendors to extend your core capabilities?
- How do you vet new vendors?
- Are you looking for new vendors now to solve current/future problems?
- Who manages your vendor relationships?

What is the process? If they answered "yes" to any of the above questions, you need to dig deeper.

Sample questions:

- Can we discuss your process of evaluation?
- Who is involved in the process?
- May we discuss your budget process?

Who oversees? And because there is always someone in charge, you'll need to speak with them.

Sample questions:

- Can you provide an introduction to ...
- Do you know of anyone else involved that we may have missed?
- Any product champions?
- Any slow adapters?
- Who has the budgetary authority to purchase?

5. Emerging & Evolving Care-delivery Models

New organizations and care delivery models are being created all the time in an attempt to reduce costs while increasing patient care and improving outcomes. Accountable Care Organizations (ACO) are but one of these types. Management Service Organizations (MSO) is another type of model being used by hospitals to assist providers in running their practices. As these new models evolve, so too will the demands of your customers. Make sure that you too are staying on the cutting edge.

Sample questions:

- Are you looking at ACO/MSO adoption?
- Where are you in the process?
- Are your partners identified?
- Are your technology needs identified?
- Can we assist you in quantifying your technology needs?

Meet the Physician Liaison

There was one individual listed above that you may not have heard too much about previously; that is the physician liaison. Hospitals typically have a person whose job is to make sure providers are happy with the service the hospital delivers. They function as a combination sales rep/problem-solver to make physicians happy and more willing to keep referring their patients to their hospital. Even though they are not buyers, they are your kindred spirits in terms of what they do. You sell your company's services to the hospital, they sell their hospital's services to the provider.

They should be on your radar anytime you have a product or service that can improve the hospital/physician relationship. Get to know them, find out what the doctors and their staffs are unhappy about. The use this information to craft relevant messages that show the doctors or the hospital purchasing team how your product solves the problem. You'll be a hero to everyone.

The title for this position may vary from place to place. Terms like physician liaison, physician/hospital relationship coordinator, outreach coordinator or something similar is the most common. In smaller hospitals, the function may be a part of community relations or marketing department or one person could be doing it all. Very few sales reps take the time to seek out the physician liaison as many are unaware the position exists. Make sure that you don't overlook this potential opportunity.

CALL TO ACTION

The purpose of this and the previous chapter was to help you lay the foundation for understanding both medical practices and hospitals. Remember, while every organization is different, there are still many similarities. By first understanding what is similar, you can begin to approach your customers more efficiently and engage them on a much higher level. At that point you'll need to adapt and tailor the remainder of your sales efforts to meeting their unique and specific problems.

For now, another good place to start implementing Pyrametrics into your sales repertoire is by taking a serious look at how you prepare for each conversation. Do you have an objective for each encounter? Do you know where you're leading the customer? Are you ready to overcome any objections? Do you have a Plan B? Success in healthcare sales is all about preparation. In the next chapter we shift gears somewhat and begin to look at your company's greatest asset, you.

CHAPTER 6

CHANGING YOUR PERSPECTIVE

"Your attitude, not your aptitude, will determine your altitude."
- Zig Ziglar

By now you should have a clear picture of what makes the healthcare industry unique, how it functions, as well as the tremendous potential it offers sales professionals. You've learned how to apply Pyrametrics to understand your market and customers, and the importance of preparing diligently for each encounter. Now we'll use Pyrametrics to assess yourself and your own likelihood for success in healthcare sales. It takes a special kind of person to succeed in this industry. You need to be just such a person. After all, if you're not on top of your game and ready to perform at the highest level, someone else will be.

This chapter is not designed like a cookbook. There is no list of ingredients that every sales rep must possess in order to be successful. Lists are far too limiting and many a successful person has defied all lists to widely exceed expectations. Instead this chapter is designed to make you think analytically, to evaluate actions and draw parallels between past and future performance.

Pyrametrics is as much about the *why* of selling as it is the *how*. One of the essential skills necessary for sales success is to be able to look beyond what your customers say and instead focus on what they do. It means looking at past performance as a predictor of future behavior. Because the more you know about what they do and why, the better you'll be able to sell to them. Interestingly, the same things apply to you. The more you know about yourself, the better able you'll be to predict your own success. And I think you'll find this a very valuable skill.

ASSESSING YOURSELF

Step I - Know What's Expected of You

As you read though the following pages, keep in mind that not only do you want to assess your own skills but you want to make sure that your skills match the needs of the industry. The healthcare industry is unique and complex, just like the people who work in it. If you're going to be successful in this market, you first need to develop relationships with your customers. And as you know, relationships start with finding common ground.

When it comes to healthcare, the tie that binds the entire industry together is the commitment to patient care. This commitment comes in many forms; caring, compassion, hard work, honesty, integrity, confidence and sound judgment are just a few. Your customers demonstrate these things each and every day. Regardless of what your function is within this market, if you're not committed to patient care, or if you can't demonstrate that commitment, then you'd best find a job elsewhere.

Step II - Understand How the World Sees You

I'd be willing to bet that there's a disparity between how you view yourself and how the rest of the world views you. You may think that you are the absolute bomb; that the world revolves around you. On the other hand, you may be a little short on self-confidence and never truly realize how valuable you are and how wonderful others consider you to be. Having the ability to see yourself through the eyes of others is a very valuable skill to have, and one that is essential for success. Great sales people are masters of self-assessment. They are constantly refining their behavior to be more effective. They see failure as temporary, and are always prepared to learn from their mistakes.

A vital part of the self-assessment process is knowing whether or not folks would ever want to buy from you. Do you have the skills to win these customers over, to get them to know, like and trust you and to form lasting relationships? This is pretty important stuff and believe it or not just making the effort to learn it is something few folks really ever do, so you're already headed to the front of the line.

You may be asking, "Why is that?" The answer is simple. Most people are afraid to seek out another's assessment of them because they are scared of the possible results, or they fear what that individual may think of them for even asking the question. If you find yourself paralyzed by either (or both) of these concerns, then the best advice is for you to close this book right now and run, don't walk into another line of work. The simple truth is that successful salespeople neither fear nor ever take personally what others think of them because they are confident in their morals, values, professionalism and capabilities. And they know that since information is the most prized commodity out there the surest (and often the only) way to get it is by asking relevant questions.

As you ask others to assess you, don't be surprised if their impressions are different than yours. They may even be substantially different. This is not only common but it's also beneficial in that it affords you a great opportunity to ask even more questions and probe into something, that while potentially unsettling, could do you an awful lot of good. If someone thinks you're not a particularly hard worker, for example, then you really need to understand why. You don't want a bad reputation to fester, particularly if it's something you can fix easily. One of the most common reasons for professional failure is that folks often can't or won't accept that others don't hold them in the same regard as they hold themselves. They are unwilling to accept another point of view, and as a result they don't change the bad or self-destructive behavior. Situations like this rarely end well.

Therefore, never be afraid to ask sharp, pointed and direct questions. If you can learn to feel comfortable doing this, especially when the topic is you, then it will be much easier (and more comfortable) to do this later on. Furthermore, with maturity comes the ability to take constructive criticism for what it really is – a tool for your own self-improvement. So go for it. Put yourself out there and don't be afraid of the results. You just might find that you really are the bomb. Whatever you learn though, positive or not, you will be on your way toward maturity, solid professional growth and success as a sales professional.

Step III - Understand Yourself

Everyone has read the story of the athlete, soldier, politician, entrepreneur or *Average Joe* who, despite overwhelming odds against them, surpasses all expectations to achieve amazing success. After just reading this and the previous section it may seem that the two are contradictory. After all you might ask, "Why should I go out and solicit someone's opinion if it is likely to be wrong?" Actually, they both go hand in hand because all types of success share one thing in common - motivation. And motivation can sometimes be very hard for others to see and assess in you.

Motivation is a funny thing. Everyone has their own means for getting things done and they're usually unique. Often times all that it takes for someone to find motivation is to be told that they can't or never will accomplish something. For others they don't need anyone else, they just find the means from some place deep within and move out. So then how do you best reconcile your own personal opinion of yourself and that of everyone else without getting bogged down?

The simple answer to that complicated question is this: The mature individual both requests and appreciates constructive criticism and sees it for what it's worth but, at the end of the day, they rely on their own internal motivation and belief in themselves to get the job done. This is particularly relevant in sales because so much depends on your own internal motivation. So if you truly believe in yourself and your abilities, then it really doesn't matter what people think. All that matters is what you think and what you know you can accomplish.

As you make the transition from where you are now to successful healthcare sales professional remember always that there will be detractors and obstacles all along your path. Armed with both a firm belief in yourself and a wellspring of motivation will get you from where you are to where you want to be.

Step IV - Develop the Proper Perspective

Did you ever shoot baskets in the driveway when you were a kid? I did. I could hit from anywhere – under the tree, near the garage, next to the sidewalk. In my driveway, I was Kobe, Shaq and Michael Jordan, all in one. If you asked me to rate my skills in the driveway, I would tell you that I could hit a jumper, sink a free throw or make a layup, no problem. But when it came to actually playing a game on a real court with defenders in my face, things were different. I could still play, but nowhere near as well. If you asked me to rate my skills in that environment, where it really counted, my answer would have been a lot different.

Plenty of sales trainers and books list the personality traits top sales performers share – persistence, enthusiasm, resilience, confidence and so on. You probably have a list of your own or you can come up with one in a matter of seconds. But there is an inherent problem when looking at a word on a list and deciding if it applies to you: Your assessment may be wrong, especially without the proper perspective. After all, how accurate are most of us when assessing our own capabilities? It's very easy to confuse a skill that we would like to have with one we actually possess. Unfortunately, sales success doesn't require just a skill or two performed independently but rather a blend of many different skills and characteristics all used in concert. It's practically impossible for you to determine if you have that right blend by simply picking words off a list. So what can you do?

Before you can accurately predict future performance, such as success in a strategic sales career, start with the right perspective. Consider what you've already accomplished and go from there. Ben Franklin wrote, "Well done is better than well said." Therefore, if you want to be accurate with your own personal assessment, forget about trying to match up individual terms on a list and instead look at your history. It might surprise you.

Here's an interesting exercise for you to consider. I included this because we're talking about perspectives. I wanted to get you to really start thinking about what you've done and its possible relevance to sales. You may have all the traits of a great salesman but never know it because not all great sales people push products. Some phenomenal sales people just go about their days never realizing what great gifts they have.

What follows is a not psychologist-certified exam, you won't see it on Dr. Phil and there's no score at the end. Just read the questions, pause, and answer them to yourself. And when you're finished, perhaps your perspective will have changed a little too.

Did you ever run a marathon?

Running a marathon is a pretty unnatural activity; people are not set up to head out and run 26 miles, at least not without a lot of preparation. To most people, just the thought of running such a race is intimidating enough. For others it's the daunting training schedule that gives them pause. Still others wonder if they'd even survive.

Few things really test your determination and motivation like training for and then running a marathon. You may be asking why it matters to someone selling into the healthcare market. Let me try and explain. I've never run a marathon myself but I've watched my wife run many. Probably the most impressive part about the whole thing is that marathon running is something you have to do completely on your own. OK, she goes out and runs with her buddies and I'm sure that helps, but it's still up to her to get out there day after day and execute. Not only that but she has to eat well, sleep well and plan out her training schedule. And she has to do it come rain or shine. It's like having a job.

Now think of what it takes to excel in sales. When you get right down to it, you're pretty much on your own, too. Certainly you have a support structure and resources that you can use when necessary, but at the end of the day it is you out there knocking on doors and making calls. You also have to plan your days efficiently, and stay proficient with academic and professional requirements. If you aren't motivated to make it happen, it's not getting done. And if you're wondering about unnatural activities, imagine a job where you have to keep calling on folks, many of whom keep telling you no, but you nevertheless have to figure out a way to get them to buy something.

Furthermore, just as marathon running is physically taxing, selling can be equally as taxing mentally. Sometimes it can takes months to close a deal. That means you have to keep moving forward, day after day, until it's finished. What's more, you may have several deals in the works all at the same time, which can get really challenging.

If you haven't run a marathon, don't worry about it. Instead look at some of the big projects that you have completed. Think about the times that you set a goal, planned for it and then executed it without asking others for help. If you recall these events fondly, and with pride, you may be just what that sales manager is looking for.

Have you ever run for public office?

This is an easy question: The answer is either yes or no. If you have run for public office, the question of whether you have what it takes to succeed in sales is settled. You do. Running for office requires the highest form of sales skills. After all, you're not selling a service or a piece of equipment, you're selling yourself. Politics is like sales on steroids. If you answered yes to this question, feel free to jump ahead to the next chapter. If you answered no, stick with me.

The reality is that most people have not been nor ever will be a candidate for public office. If you fall into that category, it may help to understand why. If you don't have the time, the resources or think all politicians are slimy, that's one thing. But if you really think you'd be a good senator, representative or even school board member and you still don't run, it's time for some serious introspection. What's holding you back?

Is it the hours? During campaign season, politicians work virtually all the time. A good sales rep will do the same. Politicians are willing to go where the voters are. Good sales reps do that, too – they join and actively participate in Rotary, Kiwanis and other service clubs, professional associations and chambers of commerce.

Do you not like speaking to strangers? Politicians talk to any and everybody. So do top sales reps. They thrive on meeting new people and they are absolutely fearless when it comes to speaking in front of groups. They know the more folks they can persuade to share their opinions, the more successful they'll be.

Are you uncomfortable when meeting with groups of disparate people? Just as a politician must answer questions on a wide range of subjects from people whose perspectives are as varied as their questions, sales reps in the healthcare industry will find themselves dealing with physicians, engineers, administrators, financial executives and even clerical support staff – all of whom have their own questions, interests and stake in the issue at hand. Successful reps, like successful politicians, have the ability to move effortlessly from topic to topic while staying relevant and interesting to each audience.

Do you resist having to state your case and defend it? Politicians are routinely asked to state and defend their positions on abortion, gay marriage, public prayer, taxes and more. Sales reps have it a little easier; they just have to be able to clearly explain why their product is better than the competition and why the price is worth it.

How do you respond to criticism? Politicians get hammered every time they speak or don't speak, every time they act or don't act. Again, it's not quite as rough on sales people, but you need to be able to accept criticism, sort out what has value and what doesn't, use what you can and let the rest roll off your back. Just as some people simply don't like politicians for any number of reasons that may or may not be valid, some people feel the same way about sales reps. If you don't have a thick skin, you probably aren't cut out for a career in sales.

Have you ever coached a team?

This is another easy question: either you have or you haven't. Successful team coaching requires a number of attributes that are essential to sales. This applies whether it's a sports team, debate team or some other kind of team. If you have coached a team, it's a good bet you are:

Organized: Coaches have to keep a lot of balls in the air at the same time, including game schedules, practices, administrative work, personality issues and potential disputes. As a sales rep, you must be able to keep the sales cycle moving while you simultaneously deal with production, delivery, maintenance, service, meetings, administration and more.

Strategic: Just as every opposing team is different, so is every customer. And just as coaches must be able to develop winning game plans, sales reps must be able to craft winning account strategies tailored to each customer.

Motivational: Good coaches know how to inspire their players to perform at their peak while fostering a team spirit at the same time. They excel at getting people to do what they don't want to do or what they don't think they can do. Top salespeople understand human behavior; they figure out what drives the people they deal with. They know how to overcome resistance with a delicate mix of persuasion and cajoling (often involving multiple decision-makers and influencers) to take the action that fits the sales strategy. Effective coaches get everyone marching in the same direction; successful sales reps do that, too.

Have you ever gone to court and won?

This question is a little trickier. I'm not asking if you ever did something wrong, got arrested, hired a fancy lawyer and beat the rap. I'm asking if you ever felt wronged, filed a suit small claims court or in other ways took action against the offending party, and won. If the answer is no, is it because you've never been wronged, or because you didn't want to take on the fight.

Top sales performers are energized by challenges. They're articulate, analytical and logical. They know, as trial lawyers do, how to get their point across effectively multiple audiences using multiple media. They are able to visualize the process, understand what needs to be said to get the message across, anticipate and overcome objections, and articulate their case so it flows smoothly from beginning to end. Most important, they trust their instincts and believe in themselves. Do you?

How good looking is your partner?

Yes, you read it correctly. And no, I don't mean to be superficial or sexist and please forgive the political incorrectness. I do have a relevant point to be made about selling.

There is a certain aura that surrounds very attractive people and a bit of mystique too. I'm not making this up. If you don't believe me just turn on the television, go to a movie or pick up a magazine; everyone is attractive. Appearance has become so ingrained in our culture that we spend billions of dollars on creams, lotions and cosmetic surgery, all to try and bring us closer to that elusive goal.

So, if you're a guy and you have your sights set on someone very attractive, you're in for an uphill battle. If you're a lady with similar ambitions, you probably have to contend with that little voice in your head telling you what a foolish idea this is. Whoever you are, trying to land the hot date is never easy and it seems to get harder the better looking they are. That might not seem fair but that's the way it is. In reality though, a lot of the difficulty is really just in your mind. Yes, putting yourself out there is uncomfortable. And yes, it makes you vulnerable. It's unanimous that no one likes rejection. That's why most people never try and just throw in the towel.

That's most people, but not all. There are some who know the answer will always be no if you don't try and that one yes makes up for a hundred rejections. Those folks are not worried about auras or mystique and they don't feel intimidated either. They feel that since attractive people want to go out too, they have no better option than going out with them. Are they plagued with insecurity, hardly.

Sales is very much about overcoming inhibitions and intimidations, particularly in the healthcare sector. There are a lot of very smart and successful folks in the industry and they can be rough on sales people. But there's no time to worry about rejection because as you're sitting by idly coddling your ego, the winners are out closing orders. Top sales people know there is no success without effort and they definitely believe you have to shoot before you can hit something. They possess supreme self confidence in themselves and their products, and believe (rightly) that theirs is the best solution.

Interestingly around the time I was writing this chapter, I chanced to hear a discussion on sports radio. The host was interviewing an agent and they were discussing some of the criteria general managers use in selecting players to draft. One of the points they consider, believe it or not, is how attractive the player's significant other is. When the host asked why, the agent replied that it demonstrates guts and shows an attitude of confidence and invincibility. Those are apparently some very valuable attributes in the sporting world.

They're very valuable attributes in the sales world too.

IT'S ALL ABOUT ATTITUDE

One day, when I was working as a technical sales rep for Hewlett-Packard, I received a lead from a professor in the Chemistry Department at a local college. The lead mentioned that the professor was looking to outfit a new lab and wanted some guidance right away. I called him immediately and made an appointment for the following day.

As I got to the department office I was stopped by a gentleman claiming to be the administrator who told me that I was not allowed to visit any professors at that time. Furthermore, he told me that all appointments were to be made through him and that when the time came to solicit vendors that he would be the one to do so. After that, he said my meeting was canceled and sent me packing.

By that time, in addition to graduating from a college, I had also called on a number of them. It was always my impression that administrators worked for the professors and not vice versa. I always thought that it was the professors who obtained the grant funding money and so they're the ones calling the shots when it came to purchasing equipment. I was also confused why a professor would request to see me if he wasn't allowed to do so.

I remember thinking, *something's rotten in Denmark.* Who is this administrator guy and why is he dismissing me like I'm some beggar selling pencils? I'll admit the whole situation made me mad. I didn't appreciate the treatment and I was not about to lose out on an opportunity. So before leaving I asked the receptionist where the professor's office was. She pointed over her should and said, "It's down at the end of the hall on the right." I thanked her and left.

But instead of leaving the building I immediately took the stairs to the floor below. Once there I walked to the end of the hall, went up the back stairs and entered the department from the rear entrance. I was lucky that the professor's office was right next to the stairs. I opened the door, walked in and found him sitting at his desk. After that we had a great meeting and about an hour later I walked out of his office with a $45,000 order.

When it comes to selling, your attitude is everything. Great sales people simply will not be denied and they continuously come up with new and more effective ways to get the job done, even if that means taking a few risks. Over the years I've told this story to many different people and their reactions have been fascinating. The most important person I told this to was my sales manager at the time.

Tom Nebel, my old HP sales manager, is good old boy from the Missouri hills. He's quick with a smile and a slap on the back, and if you give him the chance he'll talk your ear off. But there is a steely resolve about Tom that was undoubtedly born in the skies over Viet Nam. He's got the right attitude and he knows that opportunities don't come along every day. After getting back to the office, I told him about my call at the university. He listened to my whole story, never saying much until I got finished. Then he really surprised me.

"Bubba" he said, "I know all about this. The administrator saw you leaving down the back stairs and called me to complain." I guess the look on my face was priceless. I thought I was about to get reamed, but that never happened. Instead, he smiled at me and told me I had done the right thing. Furthermore, I got a commendation and my story was written up in the HP newsletter. I was lucky. It could have gone the other way and with a different manager, it would have. But sometimes you have to weigh the pros and cons and just take a chance. Success is all about taking risks and if you want to be successful then your attitude has got to be, *I may lose a little, but I can win a lot.*

There has been much written about confidence and conveying the proper attitude. Perhaps you may have actually studied the topic yourself. My experience is not based on a literature review but on personal inspection. For over two decades I saw attitude in action almost every day.

Think about the last time you went to the doctor or hospital. You might have been the patient or there supporting someone else, it doesn't matter. Remember what happened when the doctor came into the room? There could have been twenty other people in there with you but as soon as the doctor walked in everyone froze. Why is that? Because the doctor is the authority and they command respect.

People are programmed to defer to authority, real or imagined. They just are. It starts in childhood and is reinforced all the way through adulthood. It happens with doctors. It happens with teachers. It happens with coaches. It happens with policemen. It pretty much happens with anyone perceived as being an authority in their field. And yes, believe it or not, it should happen with you, too. Why? Because you are the expert in your discipline. No one knows what you know better than you do. That is what you must believe. That is the attitude you must convey.

This does not mean that you want to be cocky. I want to make that very clear. Confidence is contagious. Cockiness can be obnoxious. Sometimes the most highly regarded people are the most quiet and reserved. They let their experiences speak for themselves. And just like the super attractive folks we mentioned above, successful people have their own aura and mystique as well. Think of some super-successful people you know. Now try and tell me they don't radiate confidence. I won't believe you. Confident people stand out. You can see them a mile away. You can be that way too.

More Than a Job

Healthcare sales is a challenging occupation for numerous reasons. It's not like shooting baskets in the driveway, but rather it's more like a professional basketball game against skilled competitors with screaming crowds. There's a lot going on all at once. Can you apply all your skills in the right combination when it really matters?

In many ways, a sales career is a lot like being an entrepreneur or small business owner. Certainly you have to function within the guidelines of the company you work for, but you'll likely have a degree of independence and autonomy that most employees only dream of. Salespeople are usually some of the highest-paid people in their organizations, often earning as much or more than senior managers, junior executives and the physicians they call on.

These great benefits don't come easy: Sales is not a nine-to-five, 40-hour-a-week job. It's a 24-hours-a-day, seven-days-a-week commitment. It's making yourself available when your customers need you, whether that's early in the morning, late at night or on weekends. It's differentiating yourself from others in the marketplace through a variety of strategies designed to demonstrate your superior knowledge and abilities. It's staying current on general industry issues along with specific product matters so you're never surprised by something a customer says.

This is not to say that you'll never take time off. Personal time, family time and vacations are essential for people to stay healthy, balanced and effective. But even when they're not officially working, sales superstars pay attention to their business so they never miss an opportunity.

...

Do They Know Your Name?

Savvy politicians know that it takes an average of 13 exposures for a potential voter to remember your name, not necessarily to decide to vote for you, but just to at least remember your name. Those exposures can come in the form of personal meetings, phone calls, signs, bumper stickers, TV and radio ads, public debates and so on. It's important to mix the media up so voters don't get so familiar with the message that they tune it out.

Athletes call this approach muscle confusion, which is a training principle based on the fact that when the same stress (exercise) is continually applied to muscles over time, the muscles acclimate to the specific stress (exercise) and the activity is becomes ineffective. Variety is essential for continued results.

The sales equivalent to this is to make sure your customers never forget your name by keeping it in front of them in a variety of ways. Imagine that your customer has a little bucket in his brain with your name in it – a bucket with a hole in the bottom. To keep it from running dry, it needs constant filling. The challenge is that all of your competitors are trying to keep it filled with their name, just as you want to keep it filled with yours.

Top sales professionals keep their names in front of their customers in a systematic way using a variety of contact methods, including emails, phone calls, notes, shared information and meetings. Each contact is purposeful and has value, and differentiates the leaders from the rest of the pack.

CUSTOMERS WANT TRUSTED ADVISORS

Healthcare professionals have a unique perspective on the issue of trusted advisors because that's their role with their patients. The customers in today's health industry don't want to be *sold* anything, especially from someone they view as a hit-and-run sales rep who is only in it for the commission. Instead, they want to make a choice to purchase a solution for an issue that is important to them from someone they see as a trusted advisor, who puts their needs first.

They buy from individuals who help them identify issues and collaborate with them to find solutions – even when those solutions don't always include the sales rep's product.

It's not enough to just say that you're a "solution seller." Just about every company positions itself as a solution provider. The difference is personal and being more relevant than the rep with the competing product. When your customers believe you are sincerely focused on their best interests, not just making a sale, you will become a trusted advisor and your sales will skyrocket.

Now that you understand what it takes in the way of skills and personality to succeed in healthcare sales and how to apply Pyrametrics to your own analyses, let's turn our attention back to your customers. The more you learn about them, the more you'll be able to determine their motivations. And once you understand what drives someone, you have a virtual crystal ball you can use to predict future actions. Let's take a look at why things are done as they are in the world of healthcare and what that means to you.

CHAPTER 7

STAYING FOCUSED

"If You Can Keep Your Head When All About You Are Losing Theirs..."
- Rudyard Kipling

It's doubtful that Mr. Kipling had healthcare sales in mind when he penned those words in 1895, but they are certainly applicable nonetheless. At the time of this writing the healthcare industry is in turmoil and will likely continue to be for the foreseeable future. As we mentioned before, chaos for some means opportunity for others. Now is the time for you to really put forth the effort to excel.

But your job may not be easy. The healthcare industry, like any other, has its share of characters, all with their own peculiarities and idiosyncrasies that you'll need to figure out how to work with and work around. As you meet more and more customers always remember your place on the team and the value you bring to the table. Stay focused, remain confident and work diligently toward a well thought out goal. In the end you'll be the one to shine.

NAVIGATING THE MINEFIELDS OF EGO, POWER AND POLITICS

In the previous chapter we discussed three important points. They are:

1. Adjust your perspective - Open yourself up to looking at things in a different way and when it comes to evaluating others (including yourself) consider actions over words.

2. Adopt the proper attitude - Success is as much a state of mind as it is a result of actions. Know that whatever you want to achieve can be achieved if you first believe in yourself. And never let anyone knock you off course.

3. Look past the *How* to the *Why*. In sales as in life, train yourself to understand why something was done, not just that it was done. You will gain insight into future behavior.

In this chapter, we'll take these same points and expand on them further. We'll not only reinforce the need to possess the proper attitude, but show you why it so important maintain it. We'll discuss more about customer behavior including the reasons behind it and why understanding it is so beneficial. Lastly, we'll further describe the real environment of the healthcare market and provide insights as to how you can master working within it.

There's an old joke that introduces this section far better than anything I could come up with on my own - *Do you know the difference between God and a doctor? God doesn't think he's a doctor.*

When it comes to peculiarities and idiosyncrasies, no other industry can top healthcare in terms of inflated egos, power trips, political games and other shenanigans. If you can't keep your head in this arena or are not prepared for it, then you're in for some long days. However, if you do get it and can stay focused in the midst of it, then your chances for achieving your sales goals will soar.

One of the biggest challenges for new and even established healthcare sales professionals is the intimidation factor. Just about every culture reveres healthcare providers, particularly doctors. As the saying goes, plenty of doctors are guilty of "believing their own press" – meaning that they allow the fact that society puts physicians on a pedestal to pump up their opinions of themselves and develop attitudes ranging from moderately superior to offensively arrogant.

Of course, physicians aren't the only people you're going to be dealing with who could have over-inflated egos. There are plenty to go around. While every sales landscape has its share of rocks and potholes, many sales professionals agree that healthcare providers are some of the most intelligent yet demanding and difficult types of customers. Calling on them can be extremely stressful.

One of the common traps that inexperienced or less self-assured reps fall into is allowing others to undervalue their services. And when reps allow themselves to feel inferior and insecure, their effectiveness drops like a rock. Remember, selling is as much of a mindset as it is a skill set. If you don't believe in yourself, why should anyone else believe you? No one wants to buy from someone who lacks confidence.

Through your own behavior and attitude, it is you who sets the standard by which you will be treated – not only in your professional environment, but in your personal life as well. The key to establishing solid, effective business relationships is to consistently demonstrate and demand respect from everyone you deal with.

Regardless of your industry, you'll find people who are condescending and demeaning to sales reps, but it seems (at least anecdotally) that the issue is quite prevalent in healthcare. In my 20 years in medicine, I have seen countless examples of disrespect directed toward salespeople. You may be wondering why this is. Well like most things, the reasons are usually multifactorial.

Part of the reason for their disrespectful treatment is due to the sales reps themselves. As was covered previously, sales people don't always prepare adequately for their encounters with healthcare professionals and by doing so they portray themselves as more of a waste of time than a value-adding resource. I can't underestimate how important this is. No provider likes to have their time wasted by an inconsiderate rep who hasn't done their homework.

It's also no secret that a few industries within healthcare have demonstrated some less than stellar behavior over the years. There have been indiscretions by the pharmaceutical industry, for example. When this kind of thing happens often, it is the sales force that gets tarred with the same brush even though they may not have done anything personally to deserve it.

Another good example of guilt by association is in the health insurance business. Providers generally hold this industry in very low regard. While they see insurance as a necessary product, they also feel frustrated by the endless red tape and bureaucratic hassles that they are subjected to in order to merely to get paid. It is quite possible that Gandhi, were he to have been in the insurance business, would himself be looked upon with similar disdain.

Other reasons arise from the providers themselves. One example has to do with the differing perspectives of physicians and business people. This is changing a little bit nowadays but in general, physicians have always seen their profession as somehow above or more noble than traditional business and for that reason, they see sales people as running counter to the values and ideals that they hold dear.

Regardless of the reasons, bad behavior is often perpetuated because people generally prefer to avoid confrontations. Many sales reps are either unwilling or unable to stand up for themselves or reverse the situation; others simply accept belittling as one of the hazards of the job. But when you accept rude, disrespectful conduct from your customers, you are doing a disservice to both them and yourself.

Once an unequal relationship has been established, it's very hard to change. Even if you are successful at making a sale, you're not likely to have the degree of comfort and trust that you need for the long-term. That's why you should manage the relationship to make certain it develops properly from the beginning. Assume that you'll be treated with respect. If you aren't, make it clear that you won't tolerate anything less. I understand that this may be easier said than done, but it's not impossible. It takes courage and confidence, as was demonstrated by a pharmaceutical rep I knew.

She was walking through a hospital when she saw two physicians from a large medical group she'd been calling on for years. One she knew well and had done business with; the other she had seen but not actually met. The first physician extended his hand and greeted her warmly. When she turned to the other and extended her hand, she was shocked when that doctor put his thumbs in his ears, closed his eyes tightly and shouted "blah, blah, blah" while wiggling his fingers back and forth. Then he laughed.

Calmly and firmly, she put her hand on the physician's shoulder and guided him a few steps away from his colleague. In a low but precise tone, she said that the behavior he had just exhibited was completely unprofessional and that he should never address her in such a manner again. Did that doctor immediately become her best customer? No. In fact, they never had any significant business dealings. But the doctor was never disrespectful again, and the way she handled the situation also showed the first doctor that she is a professional who is entitled to respect.

Of course, not all forms of intimidation are so overt. Addressing the more subtle techniques customers use to intimidate sales reps is essential. Many reps feel that because their healthcare customers are so highly educated, they must adopt a deferential or submissive attitude.

In preparing to write this book, I had the chance to interview many sales managers. Nearly everyone told me that they do indeed instruct their reps to adopt a submissive or subordinate role when dealing with healthcare customers. In my opinion, this is the worst possible approach you can take, because it only reinforces any perceived inequality. It also makes developing a strong business relationship that much more challenging.

If you're wondering why many companies adopt this posture with their sales forces, you're not alone. I wondered that exact same thing for years. One day I set up a little research project to try and figure it out. Since the pharmaceutical industry is one the biggest perpetrators of this behavior, I looked at every contact I had within the industry and tried to learn as much as I could about their employment history. What I found was the following.

Theirs is a very defined career pathway which leads from sales rep to sales manager to marketing manager to product manager to training manager. Of course there is some variation, but in general the industry is very insular and compartmentalized, and everyone continues to reinforce to same old ideas they were brought up the ladder with. It's no wonder the chain is never broken.

Furthermore, even as many pharmaceutical companies began outsourcing their sales force training to third party companies, the situation didn't improve. While the companies are all fine outfits, even a cursory look at their management teams speaks volumes. They all came from big pharma. How can you get fresh perspectives when the people running these companies are all alumni of the same industry?

I've had pharma reps come to me almost begging me to teach them something fresh and relevant as they're sick and tired of hearing the same old company line. Yet in all of my years in clinical medicine, I never had one representative ever ask me about myself, my training or why I made the decisions that I made. My colleagues say the same things. If they had asked me, I would have told them this:

Physicians primarily, but all healthcare workers to some degree, are trained to be confident and decisive in their professional lives. Furthermore, they are expected to be able to defend their ideas against what can be very intense scrutiny. Therefore, they come to both *respect* and *expect* similar behavior from others. Reps who come at healthcare providers with a submissive or less than confident attitude, are just asking for trouble.

As a sales professional who knows how to identify issues and provide solutions, you bring a tremendous amount of value to the relationship. You have to believe that first, because if you don't, your customers never will. You might not be able to perform surgery and you might even faint at the mere sight of blood, but surgeons can't operate with their bare hands. They need the equipment you sell. Don't minimize your value – and never be intimidated by your customers.

Pharmaceutical reps bring significant value to the table. For instance, in the case of medical therapy it is the pharmaceutical reps who know the most about new drugs coming to market. They are able to provide key information to providers, along with product samples, study results and black-box warnings. This expertise is essential to the healthcare industry. Consider heart disease for example.

Currently cardiologists employ three treatment modalities to combat this number one killer of adults: surgical, interventional or medical management. Surgical therapy is the most invasive approach and commonly includes bypass, valve and other reconstructive surgeries. It's used in about a quarter of all cases. Interventional cardiology (such as angioplasty and stent placement, pacemaker placement and ablations) is far less invasive and is used in about half of heart disease cases.

The remaining 25 per cent of cases are not candidates for either surgery or interventional procedures. For those patients, aggressive treatment with cardiac drugs may be their only option. Cardiac medications are also used extensively in support of surgery and other procedures as well. So if you're in pharmaceutical sales, you are representing companies that make essential products that save lives. Doctors may not be the first to mention it, but without your products, they would have very little to offer. You can extrapolate this example to whatever sector you're in.

The reality is that reps are a very important part of the healthcare team, although it often seems to me that many don't recognize it. True sales success can occur only when both the customer and sales professional come together on equal footing. Despite whatever else is going on in your industry, you need to stay focused on the objective at all times.

The Name Game

Should you call the doctor "doctor?" The American business environment is becoming increasingly casual. Even C-level executives of major corporations are comfortable being called by their first names in business situations today. But healthcare is an industry steeped in tradition, so it's a good idea to find out how the person you're dealing with wants to be addressed.

The best approach is to tackle it upfront early. Say something like, "My policy is to address people formally by their title and last name. Is that what you'd prefer?" They may agree, or they may say, "Call me Bill."

If they agree that they want to be called by their title but then call you by your first name, you need to address it. Allowing that puts you in an inferior position. One way to deal with it is with humor, saying something like, "Oh, I guess we know each other well enough now to be on a first-name basis," and then start using the person's first name. An approach that's a little more gutsy would be to remind them that you'd agreed on a level of formality that goes both ways. Yes, it's risky, but it certainly sends the message that you expect to receive the same degree of courtesy and consideration that you're affording them.

...

On Doctors, Defiance and Decisions

When you're selling to physicians, it's important to know that the decision-making process you may be used to in the corporate world is generally unheard of in a medical group. In corporate America, when the boss says, "We're all wearing blue shirts on Fridays," everyone will show up at work in a blue shirt on Friday. Not so in a medical group. Despite the fact that most groups have a published hierarchy that's likely to include a managing partner, CEO or president, the actual authority of those "bosses" is variable.

In my old group, for example, if our president had proclaimed Friday as "blue shirt day," I can almost guarantee that most, if not all, of the partners would have showed up wearing shirts that were red, yellow, green or any other color *except* blue. Why? Because most doctors resist conforming to structure or recognizing authority. And despite what they might say to the contrary, many are extremely passive-aggressive. This is just something you'll have to learn to accept.

When you're selling to a medical group, always keep in mind Pyrametrics and the Process Management Algorithm (pg. 8); work smart and stay focused on those things that bring you closer to the sale. Just because the president of the group likes and supports what you're offering, it doesn't mean the sale will automatically close. In most groups, decisions are made by the numbers and the majority rules. While it's important to understand the org chart, it rarely holds the same significance as it would in your company. Therefore, building consensus is absolutely essential for success in this environment. The more partners you can get on your side, the better off you'll be.

HOW DID THEY GET HERE AND WHY SHOULD YOU CARE?

One of the key principles of Pyrametrics is to go beyond the *how* and look toward the *why*. Why do your customers do what they do? If you can answer that then you truly are headed for sales superstardom. Let's start at the top.

Everything that we do is done for a reason. Everything! That is as true in business as in life. The reasons may be simple or complex, but they are there. And you need to train yourself to look for them. Furthermore, we are all creatures of habit. Once we get into a behavior routine, it is very unlikely to change. That's why when it comes to understanding your customers, if you can reach a level where you can predict behavior, then you are doing very well. Unfortunately, because we are all products of our upbringing, before you can accurately predict where someone is going, you have to understand where they've been.

Right now if you're thinking this is all a lot of psychobabble, I wouldn't blame you. This stuff may seem a bit far removed from conventional sales training. But there is value if you're willing to embrace it. The reality is that you're probably locked in a very competitive struggle with other companies that are just as competent and creative as yours. If you want to get ahead, you'll have to dig deeper, work harder and prepare more effectively than they do. If you really want to connect with your customers then you'd better understand what makes them tick.

Think about this, imagine the kind of relationship that you have with your spouse, significant other or best friend. I'll bet that if you put your mind to it you can come up with many instances where you could just about predict their behavior. I know I can.

Just the other day, for example, I was picking up my kids from school. I have four of them. As we drove out of the parking lot my youngest daughter asked,

"Hey Dad, can we stop for ice cream on the way home?"

To which my oldest daughter said, "Mom won't like that."

Then my son chipped in with, "Yeah, she'll have a cow if we spoil our dinner."

And finally, my middle daughter got to the *why* with, "Cooking is really important to Mom. It hurts her feelings if we don't eat it."

The fact is that cooking *is* really important to my wife. She's an outstanding cook who's put in a lot of effort over the years to get that way. The kids know that it won't just frustrate her if the dinner's not eaten, she'll take it personally. And they know why. And because they know why, they're more inclined to relate to it and understand it. This kind of intimate knowledge should not be limited to friends or family. You can attain a similar familiarity with your customers. It might just take a little longer.

Here's another example. Several years ago I sat through a demonstration by a company looking to sell my group on their EMR. The meeting seemed to go well, everyone was paying attention but none of the physicians asked many questions. Everyone was pleasant and at the end the usual encouraging platitudes were dispensed liberally. Satisfied, the reps packed up their things and left, seemingly confident that the sales process was well on track.

Once they left the room the mood changed precipitously. It was obvious that only a few of the partners understood a word that was said. Others were hung up on pricing or mired in trying to make sense of all the technical minutia. No one at all seemed pleased with the presentation. In the end we went with someone else.

Not long after we closed with another vendor I received a call from the sales manager of the previous company. He seemed quite incredulous that we had gone a different way. He asked me what had gone wrong. The first thing I told him was that their last presentation had been far too technical. It was completely inappropriate for that venue. He responded that those features were the essential parts of their system and why it was different from the competition. It was imperative for us to know those things, he claimed. While that may have been so, I countered by telling him that his audience was a bunch of cardiologists, not HIT professionals. "If no one understood what was being said," he asked, "then why didn't anyone ask any questions?"

It was clear from this exchange that while he probably knew everything there was to know about EMRs, he knew very little about his customers. If no one, in a room full of physicians, ever asked a single question it was almost certainly because -

1. They didn't understand the information but were not about to show their colleagues that they didn't understand. Or,

2. They weren't about to disrupt the meeting so that they could be educated on what they may have felt they should have already known.

From the very first days of training, physicians are expected to find out the answers for themselves and not be dependent on others to supply their education. Furthermore, they are not about to let themselves appear inferior by looking as though they don't understand something. They also have very little patience. The moment the conversation stopped being relevant everyone's attention focused somewhere else.

Tim Wackel, sales training guru and my friend since the old Hewlett-Packard days, has a theory on this. He's even gone as far as to coin a new syndrome which he refers to as the *Hopieum Addiction*. He feels that if a rep goes into each call looking for encouraging words, that's all he may come away with. Tim says it's essential to make it easy for your customers to say no. And as he puts it, "At least then you have the objections out on the table and can overcome them sooner, rather than later." Tim's message is not only unique, it's right on target and absolutely essential when dealing with healthcare customers.

Confidence = Customer Knowledge + Environmental Knowledge + Great Relationships

Confidence is such an integral part of sales success, you not only need to demonstrate it, you must feel it down to your core. You develop that core foundation by applying Pyrametrics to each element of the confidence formula. Remember, start with the general then move to the specific. In the previous pages we have discussed how to fine tune your preparation so that you'll approach each customer from a position of strength.

Your self-confidence will play a significant role in your relationship with your customers. When you are genuinely confident (not cocky), the world will see you for what you are: a success. And because success breeds success, it will be easier to become a trusted advisor. The elements of the confidence formula are:

Customer knowledge. Your products and services are the keys to success for your customers, but only if they believe and want to buy. The more you know about your customers, the better able you'll be to craft relevant messages and position your products as solutions that will work for them.

Environmental knowledge. Sometimes your customers don't even realize they have a problem, much less recognize you as a problem-solver. Understanding the impact your products will have on your customers' environment will help you gain credibility and trust, as well as establish a need for what you have to offer.

Great relationships. One of the perks of a sales career is that if you are doing it right, you're spending your days calling on your friends. When your customers like you, they will want to take your calls and meetings. When you deliver value with each meeting, you'll be perceived as a trusted ally. The more allies you have at a customer site, the better. They will help you overcome whatever objections others may have about purchasing your products or services.

POWER: WHO HAS IT, WHO WANTS IT, AND HOW CAN YOU WIELD IT?

I'm sure you've experienced this just as I have; the customer who keeps calling you for advice, information or to "just chat". They invariably keep promising you the world, that big order, that important introduction, that great opportunity, only to deliver absolutely nothing. How frustrating is that?

One of the most important things you need to know is who has power in your customers' organizations. Many think they have it, others would like to have it and some really do have it, but only a little. How well you do could be contingent on how well you can sort this out. Power goes beyond simply the ability to say yes or no to a purchase. It includes influencing a purchase as nurses, technicians, managers and even patients often do. It also includes the power to control access to the person who will make the final decision. That's the power of gatekeepers, and you need to recognize and work with it.

Identifying power in a given organization is critical to success in selling to the healthcare industry. In addition to helping you avoid wasting your time trying to sell to someone who can't buy, it will help you become a strategic ally for individuals who want to maintain or increase their power. It will also prevent you from making a strategic mistake that could get you shut out of the organization completely.

Before you make your initial contact on a buyer, find out the institution's policies, procedures and rules for communication and contact. Call and ask to speak to someone in vendor relations. Then, as you start contacting individuals within the organization, confirm your understanding and compliance with the applicable policies. Large institutions, especially academic centers, tend to have very specific rules about how vendors can address various levels of the staff. Just because someone on a specific level wants to talk with you doesn't mean that doing so won't violate a policy – a policy they may not be even be aware of. Be respectful and honest. Say something like, "This is important to me. I don't want to make any mistakes. Can you help me so I know what I need to do?"

Remember, one of the benefits of calling on healthcare customers is that they are used to (and like) helping people. You know how it feels to help someone out. It feels good. It can be just as rewarding for someone to help you as it is for you to be helped. Use that to your advantage and never be afraid to enlist others to get what you need.

THE FLANKING MANEUVER

Sometimes it can be difficult, if not impossible, to get in front of key decision makers and influencers. This is a problem in every industry, but particularly in healthcare due to the challenges of the personalities and egos, their schedules and in some cases, their disdain for anything to do with selling. How can you overcome this formidable impediment?

In military parlance, the answer is to bypass the obstacle by moving around the flanks and surrounding the "enemy." Instead of crashing against the ramparts and failing, you surround your target and apply pressure from all sides until it finally surrenders. When you're trying to make contact with a key individual who is resisting, both the principle and execution are similar.

In situations where you are unable to access key decision makers, you need a strategy to have others do the selling for you. Let's say you've been trying to reach a key physician on the hospital committee responsible for purchasing a product you sell, but he's been dodging you. If you have solid relationships with others on the committee, they may be willing to arrange an introduction or forward information up the chain. Or they may be willing to speak in favor of your product as a solution. Or let's say you haven't been able to get through to the physician you need to see at a medical group. It's likely that the doctor trusts his nurse when it comes to patient care issues, the technologist when it comes to diagnostic accuracy and the administrator when it comes to measuring return on investment. That is why it is so important to sell through the entire organization and work with everybody. If you have developed relationships with these members of the physician's team and can communicate the value of what you are offering to them, they'll be in a position to work on your behalf.

To use the flanking maneuver, first be sure you understand who has influence over your customer, to what degree and under what circumstances. You also need to clearly understand the relationship between your allies and the target you are trying to reach. This tells you what they can realistically do on your behalf so that you don't waste your time or theirs trying to persuade them to do something they can't accomplish. Finally, give your allies a reason to help you and recognize and reward them when they do. And never, ever, forget to say thank you.

Establish Your Expertise

In all types of sales, but especially in the ego-driven healthcare arena, you should establish yourself as a visible and recognized expert in your market. Your name needs to get in front of your customers as an expert in more than traditional sales situations to build your reputation as an authority. If you're wondering why this is, the answer is simple. This is the way your customers recognize competence in their industry. The leaders in healthcare are the ones who publish, speak and participate in local, state and national events. Therefore, if you have the opportunity to polish your credentials in a similar way then you should. Your customers will recognize it and respect you for it, as well. Some of the ways you can do that include:

Informational articles: Get published in your industry's trade journals, on blogs and in any other outlet your customers are likely to read. Your articles should contain unbiased information related to the product or services you sell or address a key problem currently facing the industry.

Public speaking: Never turn down an opportunity to speak, as the benefits far outweigh the hassles. Make presentations to groups where you can share your knowledge and expertise. Ideally, the audiences of those groups should include your customers at places like medical societies, trade shows, industry functions and community or charitable events. When you are speaking, let your customers and prospects know and, if appropriate, invite them to attend the event. Nowadays, with information being so readily available, consider recording your talk and making the audio files available. Always take pride in what you do and never be afraid to share the fruits of your labor.

Op-ed pieces: These are the articles that traditionally appear in newspapers opposite the editorial (op-ed) page. They express the opinion of an author who is not associated with the paper. Healthcare is rich with topics appropriate for op-ed pieces you can write.

Social media: Be visible on professional social media forums such as LinkedIn, Focus and other sites where your customers are. Don't sell, tell. And always be willing to share information.

POLITICS: THE GAME EVERYBODY HATES, BUT EVERYBODY PLAYS

According to Wikipedia, the term politics is generally applied to the art or science of running governmental or state affairs but also applies to institutions, fields and special interest groups. It consists of relationships involving authority or power and the methods and tactics used to formulate and apply policy. In simpler language, political scientist Harold Lasswell defined politics as "who gets what, when and how."

As a healthcare sales professional, you'll need to deal with politics on two very specific levels:

1. The internal political environment of each of your customers, and how the individuals within those organizations interact.

2. The external political environment of government, regulation and public policy, and how that impacts your customers.

Understanding and working within your customers' internal political environment is a basic sales skill and a fundamental of Pyrametrics. You must learn the overall business needs as well as the individual wants and motivations of the people who are making and influencing purchasing decisions. With that information, you can meld the individual needs into group wants to reach a result where everyone wins.

Dealing with the external political environment can be more complex and sensitive. Your customers will represent all points on the political spectrum, with extremists and moderates on every side of every issue. For example, you may need to understand the impact of existing and proposed legislation on your customers' operations and be able to offer advice on how they can deal with the impact of those regulations. But you must do it without taking sides, no matter how strongly you might feel. You are not there as a political pundit – we already have Bill O'Reilly, Chris Matthews and legions of others. Nor are you there as a policy advisor. Your job is to sell.

In the end, mastering the politics of sales is a lot like playing chess. Everything you do is part of an overall strategy designed to move you closer to your ultimate goal. Just as skilled chess players are able to look at the board and see multiple moves and possibilities, you must be able to look at your sales opportunities and develop a thorough strategy that includes contingencies. When you are working within the structure and mindset of Pyrametrics, this becomes second nature.

Take the Pledge

In the blockbuster hit movie *Wall Street*, Gordon Gekko told his protégé Bud Fox, "The most valuable commodity is information." Be aware that as a sales rep in the healthcare field, much, and sometimes even all, of the information you gain from your customers is confidential. Part of your job is to keep that information private.

Many organizations ask sales representatives to sign a non-disclosure agreement (NDA) to assure that all information shared between the customer and supplier remains confidential. You should be willing to sign these agreements, but it's a good idea to have your own legal department review them first. It's also a good idea to carry your own standard NDA form with you in case a situation arises while you are with a customer where a confidentiality agreement would be appropriate. This demonstrates your integrity and professionalism, and reinforces your commitment to your customer.

With or without a formal NDA in place, you should always assume that anything you hear from a customer is proprietary and should be kept in strict confidence unless you are specifically advised to the contrary.

...

The Buck Doesn't Stop with You

Certainly you are responsible for your actions, but it's likely that you won't bear total responsibility for them. If you make a serious mistake, your employer could end up paying. It's based on vicarious liability, the legal principle that governs the extent of responsibility an employer has over the actions of their employees. It's a complicated subject that's beyond the scope of this book, but let's boil it down to this: If you ever have to stop and think about whether what you're doing is legally, morally or ethically appropriate, you shouldn't be doing it. If you have any questions about what you're considering doing or have been asked to do, check with your manager or your company's legal department.

KEEPING SECRETS, RESPECTING PRIVACY

As a trusted advisor to your customers, you will likely become privy to proprietary or other information that your customers would not want revealed to competitors. While you may be tempted to leverage that information to advance your sales, don't do it. It's unethical and can ruin your career and professional relationships.

A rep for a large HIT firm was trying to sell similar systems to two competing hospitals in a large urban market. In the process, he learned confidential information about both facilities' strategies. Instead of keeping that knowledge to himself as he should have, he used it to try to expedite the respective sales. When talking to the CIO at Hospital A, he would say things like, "If you buy this system now, you'll get a leg up on Hospital B, because they're not releasing funds until next year." He would then make similar statements about Hospital A to Hospital B's CIO based on the proprietary information he knew.

What he didn't know was that the two CIOs not only knew each other, they were friends. They quickly realized that the rep hadn't made an innocent slip; he was committing deliberate breaches of trust. To verify that, they both fed him bogus information, stressing confidentiality. When the information was shared, the two CIOs reported the situation to their respective CEOs who, in turn, contacted the vice president of the HIT firm. The rep was promptly fired.

Let me clarify that it is perfectly acceptable to discuss information about your customers' competitors when that information is publicly available. That shows your customer that you are a professional who is committed to staying current on industry information and trends. But any confidential information you learn, must be kept confidential.

Beyond the information you learn as part of the sales process, when you are conducting sales activities in an active environment where healthcare is taking place, you will likely be exposed to confidential patient information in some form. This may be as simple as seeing someone you recognize in the waiting room to overhearing conversations about an individual's condition, test results or other sensitive items. When you are in healthcare facilities and see people you know who are there as patients, let them initiate any contact. If they prefer to pretend they didn't see you, respect that. If you see or overhear anything confidential, don't react. Instead, "forget it" immediately. The consequences of sharing or otherwise using that information in an unauthorized manner could range from harmless to major, so the best policy is to not share sensitive information – not with anyone, in any context, anywhere, period. Nothing will tarnish your reputation or potentially end your career faster than if you are found to be in violation of this most basic rule.

Here's an example of a situation you might encounter. In today's world of cell phone cameras and instant access to the internet, it's easy for private information to quickly become very, very public – and sometimes the person who reveals the secret does it accidentally and innocently. A sales rep who had been calling on a plastic surgeon for several years ran into a friend he hadn't seen in a long time in the doctor's waiting room. The two had a brief chat, promised to stay in touch, and on a whim the rep asked the receptionist to take a picture of the two of them with his cell phone. He uploaded the picture to a social media site, tagging himself, the doctor's office and his friend. He didn't notice that another patient had been caught in the background of the picture, and her image was clearly visible in the photograph that was identified as being in a plastic surgeon's office. She did not want the fact that she was having cosmetic surgery to be common knowledge, and she initiated legal action against both the physician's office, the sales representative and his company. Even though she was never identified in the photo and it was immediately taken down when she complained, she eventually received a financial settlement from the doctor and the sales rep was fired.

There may be times when you have a valid business reason for taking photographs in a medical facility. It's essential that you be sensitive to everything that's in the picture and control the availability of the image. By everything, I mean more than just the people. An equipment rep was taking some snapshots of a heart catheterization lab for his team to use to put together a proposal for the facility. The rep didn't notice that the monitor in the room hadn't been reset and had a patient's name and personal information on the display.

Fortunately, the images were not widely distributed; the rep wasn't fired, but he was disciplined for the breach of confidentiality.

One final point on the issue of confidentiality: Don't ask employees of the medical facilities you're calling on to violate the rules. I used to know a pharmaceutical rep who was close friends with a nurse who worked at a major medical group. The rep began dating a man who was a patient at the practice. She asked her nurse friend to check his file to find out his birthday (and who knows, maybe some other private information as well). As it happened, the man's birthday was a few weeks later, and the rep arranged a surprise party for her new boyfriend. When he asked how she knew his birthday, she confessed to getting it from her friend. Far from being amused by her resourcefulness, he felt betrayed and angry. He retained an attorney and within a few weeks, the rep and the nurse were unemployed – and he was looking for a new girlfriend.

Applying the Pyrametrics infrastructure will help you gain vast amounts of knowledge in a relatively short period. Knowledge may be power, but especially in the healthcare industry, it's critical that you use this type of power carefully and never inappropriately. In the next chapter, we'll look at information you can and should use to reach your sales goals and the strategies you can use to help you obtain it.

CHAPTER 8

IT'S ALL ABOUT SALES

"In preparing for battle I have always found that plans are useless, but planning is indispensable." - Dwight D. Eisenhower

Every flight, from the simplest hop in a Piper Cub to the most complex missions of the space shuttle, begins and ends with a checklist. This is because when a task is important, like takeoffs and landings, there is no substitute for having a logical, defined and methodical process to follow each time you do it. Pyrametrics provides healthcare sales professionals with just such a process.

Selling is challenging, even for the most basic goods and services. Mix in the complexity of the healthcare industry, the customers involved and the dollars at stake and there is absolutely no room for error. How can you keep it all straight?

We've already discussed the Process Management Algorithm (PMA) (pg. 8) and its relevance in keeping you focused on only those things that move you closer to the sale. But just as the PMA is a tactical tool, there is also a need for a strategic template that you can follow in each and every sales situation, one that will keep you just as focused on the big picture. That tool is the SALEs Process.

INTRODUCING THE SALES PROCESS

One of the tricks medical students use to help them remember important information is to make up catchy mnemonics that can be easily recalled. For example, as a cardiologist, one of the mnemonics I used to remember the different heart valves was *All Physicians Take Money* – *Aortic, Pulmonic, Tricuspid* and *Mitral.* It might seem banal or even a bit crass, but it worked.

When it comes to professional sales training systems, there are many mnemonics, abbreviations and catchy little terms that others have coined to help them remember key steps. Your company may have even tried a few and while all have their merits, I believe none are as simple and straightforward as the process we teach in every Pyrametrics course – a process called SALE.

SALE is the process that keeps you on task in a systematic way, regardless of how simple or complex your product or service is. SALE stands for the four key elements of any sales cycle:

- Survey
- Align
- Leverage
- Extend

When you use the SALEs process, you'll know exactly where you are at every stage of every sales cycle and you'll be able to stay on track regardless of the distractions.

Though I will explain each step of the SALEs Process, it's important to always keep in mind that this is an overlapping circular system, not a linear sequence of events that you can check off and consider done. You could very easily be at different stages of the SALEs Process with different customers within the same account.

Let's take a look at each element of this simple yet extraordinarily effective process.

SURVEY

The survey step is your advance work, and it is the foundation for everything else that happens in the sales cycle. In the tactical sense it roughly equates to the top line of the PMA. When you survey, you find out as much as you can about your prospective customer *before* you make the first contact. This allows you to differentiate yourself by demonstrating your professionalism and respect for your customers and their time. As we've mentioned previously, healthcare industry buyers are busy and they're not receptive to sales people who waste their time. Your goal is to add value at each customer encounter. Don't ask your customers to give up their time to advance your agenda; make sure you are always advancing theirs.

One of my students had been selling a long time when she took the Pyrametrics training. She said one of her early sales managers taught her this approach when calling on new accounts. At the first meeting, sit down, pull out a notebook, and say, "Mr. Customer, so that I can gain a better understanding of your business and how we can help, I'd like to ask you a few questions and take a notes while we talk. Is that okay?" The questions were very basic: What did the customer's company do? How did the sales rep's product fit? What needs did the prospect have that weren't being met? If the customer saw a better product, would he make a change?

Though that may have been an effective sales technique years ago, it likely won't work today. In fact, a rep who tries that approach today will have a hard time getting the customer to even take a meeting, and if she's successful at getting the meeting, the customer is likely to be more irritated than impressed. Why? Because anyone can sit down, ask basic questions and let the customer fill in the blanks. That approach won't work with busy healthcare professionals. From the very first contact, you have to add value to their day. You need to give them something they didn't have before. As we pointed out previously, there are opportunity costs associated with every decision, so make sure that when your customer decides to spend time with you, you make that time more valuable than if they had chosen to do anything else.

In Chapter 9, we'll talk about the nuts and bolts of proper questioning. For now, be aware that your research must prepare you to ask relevant questions, ones that convey your respect for their time and the desire to add value.

Survey Resources

Thanks to the internet, the Survey step is easier than ever, but it still takes effort to gather, sort and process the information. Keep the fundamentals of Pyrametrics in mind as you organize your research. Move from the general to the specific. You know, for example, the healthcare industry is in a state of flux. This is as true in Bangor, Maine, as it is in San Diego, California. That is your foundation. Now apply what you've learned globally to what's happening locally to what's ultimately happened with your specific customers.

Though the requirements may shift as you call on different customers, doing as much in advance as possible will help to differentiate you and give you a significant edge over the competition.

These resources are a good starting point:

Customer website: This may seem painfully obvious, but I'm amazed at how many sales reps don't bother to thoroughly check out their customers' websites before making an initial contact. Browse through every page. If it's a public corporation, be sure to check out the investor information including the financial statements and the minutes from stockholders meetings. Read any related blogs. Subscribe to the mailing list if they have one. Study the news releases. Evaluate the site from a general impression perspective and consider: Is it well-done, user-friendly and clearly put together by someone who understands internet marketing? Or is it clumsy, hard to navigate and out of date.

Most physician practices and many hospitals have biographies of their medical staff and sometimes even the senior administrators on their websites. Those bios typically include where they trained, where they worked before, significant career achievements and sometimes personal information about their family and interests. Knowing these details will make it easier for you to find common ground and develop your relationship with the individuals. We'll talk more about that soon.

In addition to the prospective customer's website, check out the sites of their direct competitors as well as other similarly respected organizations. For example, let's say you're doing research to prepare to call on Women's Hospital in Greensboro, NC. Study the websites of other hospitals serving that market, but also take a look at the websites of Winnie Palmer Hospital for Women & Babies in Orlando, Woman's Hospital of Texas and other women's hospitals. All of these things can offer you insight into your customer's world.

Competitors' website: Your customers have competition too. Make sure to glance at their websites – you don't have to study every word, but you need to know what they're doing because this information is very important to your customers. Remember, what's important to your customers should also be important to you. Furthermore, knowing about your customer's competition increases your credibility and there is nothing ever wrong with that.

Industry websites, blogs and publications: Study websites that deal with the medical industry in general and the segment that affects your product or service in particular. Subscribe to the blogs of the top thought leaders in your field. If any of your customers are blogging, try and familiarize yourself with their writings too. Nothing would impress a customer more than you quoting something they've written about.

You should also subscribe to the leading publications that cover your industry as it's almost a certainty that your customers are. This may not give you details about a specific customer, but you'll learn about the industry and the general issues your customers are facing. The websites of the medical associations in your specific state, county and even city or town may detail many of the pressing local issues that you should know about. You don't want look uninformed, particularly if they ask you about current or pressing issues.

Social media: Once you've identified the individuals you'll be contacting, learn more about them through social media. Read their LinkedIn profiles and see what groups they're in. Joining those groups will give you additional insight into your customers' professional concerns and may even introduce you to additional prospects. Don't be afraid to mine their contact list for others that you could approach. Remember, sales is all about networking. The bigger your network, the more effective you can be. Don't stop with professional information only. Check out their Facebook profiles to find out about their personal interests. Follow them or their organizations on Twitter. Every bit of information you discover is a potential connection building resource.

Keep in mind that many physicians are very cautious about using social media in order to protect their own and their patients' privacy. Non-physician care providers and non-medical staffers in medical facilities are much more likely to be found participating in social media sites. Something else to be aware of is that it's common for executives and senior managers to delegate their social media activities to an assistant or the organization's marketing department. You should still connect, but be aware that you may not actually be communicating with the person represented.

When it comes to actually connecting on social media, learn and follow the rules of online etiquette. Don't ask a complete stranger to be friends on Facebook. It's certainly more acceptable for people who've never met to connect on LinkedIn, but introduce yourself first or get a mutual friend to introduce you. A word of caution: Be wary about responding to connections suggested by the social media platforms, and don't just automatically try to connect with everyone you "might know." When I was running for office, one of my elderly patients came to the office with his daughter. Coincidentally, my volunteer social media coordinator saw the daughter on Facebook as a "person you might know" and innocently sent her a friend request, having no idea she had been in my office with her father that day. The daughter was extremely angry; she call my nurse, said it was inappropriate and a few other things that don't need repeating. Though I think the daughter overreacted, that's not the point. People will overreact to some of the most innocent things, so don't give them any ammunition.

Associations: Research the associations your prospects are involved in. This could include charities that are supported either by the individuals or the business organization, professional organizations, and civic groups, and could be local, statewide, or national. Study their websites, subscribe to their newsletters and attend their meetings.

Government agencies and resources: Just about every aspect of healthcare delivery and payment is regulated to some degree. Know the agencies that have oversight of your particular niche and stay current on what they're doing.

General online search: Do a basic online search of individuals and organizations using Google, Yahoo or Bing. Results may vary by search engine. Look for articles about the practice or hospital, articles written by the physicians and other providers, reviews of the facility and providers, complaints about issues ranging from care to billing. Go several pages deep into the search results, don't just skim the top items. Keep in mind, of course, that plenty of individuals and even companies have the same or similar name, so evaluate the information with that in mind.

People you already know: Tap into your own network for information about prospects. Most people are happy to share what they know. Of course, you need to be discreet and completely professional.

Make a phone call: There's nothing wrong with calling up a hospital or a medical group and asking questions. You may need to be a bit creative to get the information that you want, but that's okay. One of the tricks I recommend is to call and pretend to be a patient or a patient's family member. You can say that you're relocating to the area and want more information on local providers. If you're calling a hospital, ask to speak to the marketing department. If it's a medical group, one of the nurses or the administrator will gladly take your call. Don't be shy in asking about the office, the personnel, their reputation, the area they cover, what services they offer, etc. Sometimes you can get a lot more valuable information by speaking to someone.

Take a walk: Another great way to get the feel for a customer is to do a personal recon mission. Take a walk around their site. This usually works best with hospitals, particularly the large academic or community centers, but even visiting the smaller outfits can be beneficial. Doing this gives you information you just can't get over the phone and sometimes provides a unique perspective. You may see your competitors running around or catch wind of something they're up to. It may also send them a message that you're in the game too. A few harmless head games never hurt anyone.

As you do walk around don't be shy about handing out your business card and other things like product flyers or company information. Bringing food along is usually a good ice-breaker too as everyone in healthcare loves getting fed.

Cast a Wide Net

Take a broad approach to the Survey process. Don't eliminate any opportunities by keeping your focus too narrow. In addition, research all the key players in a medical practice, not just the one(s) you expect to be calling on. Remember that organizational politics are not always apparent from the outside. Expect and be prepared for the unexpected.

Use the Survey step to stay ahead of your customers in terms of identifying problems and developing solutions. That way you can get to them before they realize they need your offering and show them you understand their organization. It can be very powerful if you can discover even just one little thing that your competitor doesn't know. Then when the time comes you'll be able to guide them through the process of articulating the important issues efficiently and in the process differentiate yourself from the competition in a huge way.

What You Need to Find Out

Some of this information was presented previously but it's being mentioned again in the context of your survey in order to help reinforce the concepts and the need to always approach each account in a logical and methodical way. Therefore, we'll begin here. If your customer is a medical group, use these questions as a guide for what you should know before your first contact:

What is the focus or specialty of the practice?

Not all providers function similarly. By understanding the practice specialty (or specialties), you will gain an idea of the complexity of the organization, its dependence on technology (do they have just basic office equipment or an entire imaging center to outfit and manage?), its relationships with other groups and local hospitals and more, all of which will help you formulate an effective sales strategy.

What kind of diseases do they treat?

Knowing the medical specialties and type of diseases treated will give you insight into technology requirements, financial viability, management structure, hospital coverage requirements and call schedules.

What is the business structure of the practice?

Is it a solo practice, a small professional association or a large group? Bigger practices generally mean a greater dependence on technology and potentially larger budgets. Knowing how a practice is managed helps you identify key personnel and understand the decision making process.

What is their governance model?

Remember that while medical group may utilize the same management terminology as your company, they probably don't function the same way. Understand if possible, before you start calling, how decisions are made and by whom.

How many locations do they have?

You need to go where your customers are. If their main office is in Washington, DC but they have satellite offices in Virginia and Maryland, you'd better be in those locations as well. If you're selling technology such as telecommunications or HIT, you'll need to understand their physical organization to determine their technical requirements.

How many and what type of practitioners do they employ?

Find out the composition of the group. Is it primarily physicians, or are there nurse practitioners, physician assistants, physical therapists and other provider types in the organization?

Are biographies and photographs of the providers on their website?

Study this information so you will recognize people before you meet them and know at least some basic information about them.

Who is the practice manager and/or administrator?

Depending on the practice type, the manager or administrator may have significant power when it comes to purchasing, or none at all. You need to find out who this person is and what their role is within the organization.

Do they conduct on-site medical testing? If so, what type(s)?

You've already learned that owning and operating certain types of imaging and testing equipment can be very lucrative for the practice. Knowing what services your customers provide helps you determine which of your products and services they need. Also, groups with these capabilities often have bigger budgets and potentially greater opportunities for sales reps.

Are they active on social media?

Groups that have embraced social media and see the value of these emerging trends may be more willing to purchase products or services in support of these activities. Also, monitoring their social media sites will give you an idea of the overall complexion of the practice and its patients.

What is their reputation in the community?

How a group conducts its business could have significant implications as to how they will work with you. Groups that have sterling on-line endorsements are likely to have good relationships with their vendors. If the group has a bad reputation, proceed with caution. Sometimes the best customer is the one you didn't do business with.

Who handles their patient complaints?

If a group has assigned one person to specifically interface with patients and handle their complaints, it likely means they take the issue of patient satisfaction seriously.

Understanding the tenor of every organization you call on, in particular as it relates to how they deal with patients, partners and other suppliers, will help you get a sense of what they'll expect from you.

Remember, hospitals function much differently than medical groups. In many cases, hospitals are run by trained business professionals not healthcare providers. They often have a definite hierarchy with a structured, committee-mandated decision making process, and require a lengthy and frequently complex sales cycle. If your prospect is a hospital, you should know the answers to these questions and more before you make your first contact:

What type of hospital is it – community, tertiary, specialized, academic or government?

Each hospital type has its own complexion, decision making process, unique bureaucracy and set of hurdles that you will have to overcome.

How many hospitals are in the system?

The bigger the system is, the bigger the potential opportunity. But the challenges and sales cycles typically increase along with organization size.

What is each hospital's catch-man area?

You need to know where the hospital draws its patients from and who its competitors are.

Is it for-profit or non-profit?

As you learned in Chapter 2, a hospital's profit status may affect some of its administrative procedures.

Is there a centralized purchasing department?

You need to know if each department does its own buying or if all purchases are funneled through a central purchasing department.

Where are decisions made?

Purchasing decisions are not always made in the same location where items are used.

Are biographies and photographs of the senior management team on the website?

Study this information to build your relationships with these key decision-makers and influencers.

Where does the hospital place in various rankings?

When hospitals gain recognition for certain functions, it's a source of pride for the institution and may mean greater opportunity for you.

What is the hospital's reputation in the community?

Know how the various institutions in your territory compare with one another and use that information to develop your sales message.

For prospects that fall into other categories, such as specialty service providers, adjust the above questions as appropriate to gather a sufficient foundation of information so you can approach the prospective customer with the a level of confidence and preparation.

Reputation Matters

Your reputation as a sales professional is critical to your success. But your customers' reputations should be just as important to you as yours is to them. You need to know how they do business, make decisions and meet their financial obligations. Consider that if they provide a questionable level of care and your products are involved, you could be included in any resulting litigation. Or if they are exceptionally demanding, they may take a disproportionate amount of your time, which could prevent you from making other sales. And if they don't pay their bills, your company could take a serious economic hit. Finally, there is the issue of guilt by association. If an entity has a verifiably poor reputation, that image could reflect on suppliers. Find out everything you can about your prospects and then decide if they deserve to be your customer. Remember, sometimes the best customer is the one you didn't sign. Performing a thorough survey up front may help you sidestep these problems before they arise.

.....

Know the Rules

Before you make your first visit to an account, ask about any special procedures that might be in place for sales reps. For example, some hospitals have designated parking for suppliers. Some medical practices prefer that sales reps come in by a back door or employee entrance. You may have to pass through a security screening that you'll need to allow time for.

If you're to be accompanying a provider to the ER, ICU, operating room or procedure suites, make sure you have the appropriate permission and clearance.

If you're selling pharmaceuticals, make sure to check if the group will even see you. Many have begun to implement "no see 'em" policies where reps are essentially banned from the practice. It's good to know about that *before* you show up at the front door. Also be aware that if you're planning to bring in lunch or snacks for the providers that office policy may require you to bring enough for everyone staff and support staff included. Nothing is more embarrassing than to have to tell a bunch of hungry customers that there's, *no soup for you.*

You don't need to take up the time of a busy physician or executive to get this information. Schedule your appointment, then call back and ask an administrative person for the details. Most hospitals and many larger medical groups have individuals whose job includes interacting with suppliers. Identify these people and build a relationship with them, because they'll be a tremendous resource for you.

.....

Find the Decision Maker

Don't waste your time trying to sell to someone who can't buy. Never be afraid to ask about the decision making process. You need to know if the person you're dealing with has the authority and resources to make the purchase. If they don't, you need to find out who does.

A great way to do that is to create an account profile that maps out all the players and positions you're dealing with, then ask one or more of your contacts to verify the accuracy and completeness of your information. Set up a chart with the names and titles, along with their function as it pertains to you. Your preliminary information can be found through various public resources such as the organization's website or LinkedIn profile. Once you make contact on LinkedIn, mine their contact list to help fill in the blanks in your own records.

A while back, I was at a customer site speaking to an inside sales rep. She was lamenting that her customer profile was lacking an accurate org chart. I suggested the above LinkedIn method and by later that afternoon, she has filled in almost all the blanks. This approach really does work well. Remember, there is lot of information out there if you're willing to look for it.

ALIGN

The second part of the SALEs process is Align. This will also include first customer contact. Align is where you identify similarities, shared experiences and common goals that you can use to build your relationships on. While the most notable aligning you'll do with a customer is during your early meetings, you should continually (and consciously) align with your customers at each contact for the life of the relationship.

Remember that companies don't buy from companies, people buy from people. And they buy from people they know, like and trust. In other words, they buy from people with whom they are aligned.

Back in the 1980s, I co-owned a software company. My partners and I were in our 20s, and one night over pizza and beer, we came up with an idea to use chaos theory to model a Soviet military application. So innovative was our idea, that we managed to brief the Joint Chiefs of Staff, which was amazing for a group of twenty-something fraternity brothers. More than 20 years later, I was doing some consulting for a telecom company and had the chance to call on a retired Army colonel employed there. I learned about his military background as I was doing my Survey work, so in our first meeting, I mentioned that I had briefed the Joint Chiefs and told him about the chaos theory proposal. Though I expected him to be moderately interested, I was surprised when he said, "That was you?" He went on to say that he and other officers had heard about a small company that brought the idea to the Pentagon, but since the firm didn't have the resources to handle the implementation, the Pentagon gave the contract to a big corporation.

While it was gratifying to me personally to know that my partners and I had planted a seed that was effectively used for our national defense, it was also interesting how that conversation closed a loop that had been open for more than two decades. But the point of sharing this story is that it resulted in an almost immediate alignment between the customer and me. In doing my homework, I suspected telling that story would be an appropriate way to build a rapport. I had no idea it would have such a tremendous impact.

Of course, that's a coincidence you're not going to encounter often. But you might discover that you and the prospect went to the same school, are from the same town, have kids the same age, are interested in the same sports teams or have some other issues that will allow you to align.

This example is even more interesting. I had been trying very hard to get the attention of the training manager for this particular pharmaceutical company. I would send emails, leave messages and forward interesting articles all with the hope of making contact. Unfortunately it never worked. One day I happened to be visiting Oklahoma State University. While the host was giving us a tour of the campus I snapped a picture of their new football stadium with my cell phone camera. Then, recalling that the training manager had gone to OSU, I forwarded on the photo to him with a friendly caption. Within 45 minutes my cell phone rang. In this case the methodical survey work paid off with a great alignment. You just never know what may trigger a conversation.

A key part of the Align step is what we call small talk, an ice-breaking, informal conversation about subjects not directly related to your business purpose. While too much small talk can be a waste of time, a certain amount of it has value. When small talk is used as a conversation opener, it allows people to demonstrate their friendly intentions. In a business meeting, it helps participants get a sense of the others' reputation, level of expertise and whether or not they're even interesting to talk too. Small talk is also useful as a tool to close a conversation. It's not always necessary, but it can soften a parting that might otherwise be abrupt. Top sales performers know when small talk helps, and when it doesn't.

Interestingly, small talk doesn't just apply to sales people, it can benefit networking of all types. When I was in practice a routine 20 minute appointment would include about 10 minutes of small talk. The patients just seemed to expect it. It drove me insane because I was busy and wanted to get the show on the road, but I understood that many times patients just wanted to get the know the person who will be taking care of them. Customers can have the same expectations of their reps. Always try and get a feel for your customer's appetite for such behavior before you get started because you certainly don't want to waste their time or be perceived as frivolous or unprofessional.

When you are beyond small talk and into the meat of your discussions, you need to continually align, continually check to be sure that you and your customers are bonding as people as well as demonstrating you're understanding of their issues and the issues of their business. Aligning lets you build your mental database, something we'll discuss in Chapter 9. It lets you focus on finding solutions and solving problems, not simply on closing deals. It allows you, when appropriate, to move outside a business relationship to a more social or personal one. You cannot ever hope to become a trusted advisor if you are not aligned.

CHEW ON YOUR CUSTOMERS

Another powerful mnemonic that I developed to help you search for common ground with prospects is CHEW, which stands for children, hobbies, education and wife (spouse). During your Survey and when you Align (meet them face-to-face), look for opportunities to CHEW in a natural, friendly way. Most people – even very busy people – enjoy the chance to talk about their families and things that interest them.

Three critical requirements for effective CHEWing are:

1. Be observant. Every time you visit a customer, take note of your surroundings. A great place to find something to CHEW on is in your customer's office. There will always be something you can use to build a relationship in there sitting on the desk, hanging on the wall or resting on a book shelf.

When I first started selling at HP, I had the chance to visit a guy who ended up being a very good customer of mine. He was an engineer and the owner of a manufacturing company in northern Cincinnati. I remember being very intimidated as he walked me from the lobby to his office. But once I was there, I found many opportunities to align.

For instance, just looking at the walls gave me several things to CHEW on. First, we had both graduated with electrical engineering degrees from the same university. Next, because his company built components for military aircraft, he had several pictures on his wall, pictures that I recognized from my time as a program manager for the Air Force. When I looked at his desk I saw that he had a small Cincinnati Bengals helmet and some other sporting memorabilia. Although I was (and still am) a Vikings fan, I had season tickets to the Bengals. I knew the team very well. Finally I noticed that he had several Tom Clancy and Larry Bond books on the shelves. As a techno-thriller nut myself that just gave us more in common. You see, it is rare that you'll not be able to find something in common with you customers. Now every time I visit a customer site I make sure to look around and take good mental notes on the surroundings. The trick is to make sure to always follow up. Remember, any information is useless if you don't act on it.

2. Be honest. Don't pretend to be something you're not simply to try and connect. Don't claim to be a football fan if you've never seen a game. People are not stupid and they'll see right through you. Keep your CHEWing

conversations casual and non-intrusive. If the website doesn't mention anything about a person's family, you don't see a wedding ring or any family pictures in the office, and the prospect hasn't mentioned a family, don't ask if he has any kids. And if the prospect demonstrates resistance to a non-business discussion, respect that and move on.

3. Be vanilla. It's also a good idea to avoid topics that are controversial or potentially divisive. In healthcare, it's hard to completely avoid politics because you'll often be dealing with legislation that effects you and your customers. But it's one thing to talk about the impact of HIPAA patient privacy regulations on a medical practice's operations and altogether something else to discuss whether minors should be able to get abortions without parental consent. At any given time, there are several very hot potatoes being tossed around in the healthcare market. As a well-informed sales rep, you'll certainly know what they are and if you don't, get on it. If your customers have opinions, listen to them, but avoid taking a position that could come back to haunt you.

At the end of the day CHEWing is a very useful and powerful tool and it makes quite a good impression when you use the information in a kind, considerate and respectful manner. You can also use the information you've obtained while CHEWing to augment a robust collateral program. We'll discuss more on that later. But remember, you don't ever want to betray a confidence by using sensitive or personal customer information in an unethical manner. Doing so might not just end a friendship, it could end your employment as well.

Know the News

Although it can be fun to weigh in on a particular topic and kick it around with your customers, you have to realize why you're there and what your purpose is. Most likely you weren't hired to pontificate about the industry's most controversial topics. Instead they probably want you out building relationships and moving products. One of the quickest ways to damage both of those objectives is by coming down on the wrong side of an issue and alienating your customers in the process. Of course, everyone is entitled to their option. Unfortunately, your customers may not see the other view.

At the time of this writing there are several issues that you would be smart to know about, but shy away from engaging in any lengthy discussion over. They are:

1. The Affordable Care Act (ObamaCare) - With the reelection of President Obama, the Affordable Care Act is now law of the land. Regardless of that fact many folks still harbor strong feeling both ways. While it is possible that some of the provisions could impact your industry, you'd be smart to limit your comments to those direct areas of involvement only, and not carry on about the political points one way or the other.

2. Tort Reform - There are some who say that excessive litigation is severely impacting how care is delivered in the United States and therefore should be sharply curtailed. Others claim that litigation is a right and lawsuits serve to keep the system in check and poor providers at bay. Both sides agree that it is the lawyers who benefit the most. Regardless of how you feel about this topic, I guarantee you that someone you're calling on will be on the other side. Therefore, unless you're lobbying for the AMA or the ABA, I would stay focused on selling.

3. Specialist Pay vs. Generalist Pay - This is one of those lightening rod issues that is only going to get worse before it gets better. When it comes to reimbursing physicians in this country, there is a large discrepancy between the pay for specialists and generalists. Specialists claim that their increased training, higher risk, advanced skill set and sicker patient populations warrant higher compensation. Generalists counter by saying that if it wasn't for them to find and refer patients, the specialists wouldn't have anyone to treat, which makes them deserving of better compensation. Either way, this is NOT an issue that will be settled in a sales call. My advice, keep your eye on the order and give this issue a wide berth.

4. Gun Control - In light of the recent tragedies in Colorado and Connecticut, the spotlight has once again been turned on this topic. As with the other issues, whatever position you have will be offensive to someone you're calling on. Therefore, keep this one holstered.

5. Abortion & Women's Rights - Just like #4 above, this topic is divisive and it will continue to spark strong reactions from the opposing parties. This is not to say that you should forgo your right to free speech, but you just may not want to exercise that right during a sales call.

LEVERAGE

The Leverage step of the SALE process is when you use all the tools at your disposal to position your products and offer winning solutions. This is where you solve the problem using whatever resources you have.

Leverage can be simple or complex, depending on the circumstances. If you're supplying prescription pads to a hospital print shop, working with a single decision maker and just a few locations, you're looking at fairly simple leverage. You'll address issues related to variety, packaging, delivery schedules and pricing. You'll find out what needs the hospital has that aren't being met and then lay out a plan to meet them. Again, not rocket science.

But if you're a systems integrator looking to outfit an entire intensive care unit with specific systems capabilities, the process will be far more complex. You'll be selling across multiple departments, dealing with individuals at a variety of management and authority levels and collaborating to develop a range of solutions. It is also possible that while you are in the leverage stage with some customers that you could be aligning with or surveying others. If the process is to go smoothly, it's up to you to keep it all straight.

Use Pyrametrics to help you go from the complex to the simple. Breakdown each project into manageable tasks and work through them systematically.

Remember the PMA and try to spend your time doing on those things that will move you closer to the sale. Use the same approach in managing your contacts, internal and external resources and delivery schedules. This can be challenging work but if you can stay focused and organized chances are things will go a lot better.

Some of the Leverage resources you'll use include:

- Collaterals, including product information in the form of brochures, white papers, research reports, data sheets, YouTube videos, webinars and other media.
- Samples that allow your customers to try before they buy.
- Real-time demonstrations that show your customers what your product looks like in action.
- Specialized training that teaches your customers how to get the most out of what you offer.
- Your own tech support team and SMEs (subject matter experts) that can join you on calls to talk with your contacts or their own counterparts in the customer's organization.
- Your senior management who can help when you need C-level support.
- External consultants, hired guns, that can be brought into augment your core competencies.

The final act in the leverage is to close the sale and get the order. But this should not be attempted unless consensus has been reached and all the obstacles have been overcome. If you have been successful in following the SALEs Process to this point then the closing the sale should not be difficult. Instead, closure success should be seen almost as a by-product of a well-executed campaign. After all, once you have successfully differentiated yourself, established a great rapport, sold through the organization and overcome any objections to your stellar solution, there should be little else to do other than wait for the purchase order.

EXTEND

The final part of the SALEs process is Extend. This is where you build upon your recent successes to venture further to other opportunities. Say for example, that you recently sold a powerful financial product to a medical group. Now you can use that success as a stepping stone to other practices. Take the time to ask for referrals. Because providers are well connected with their peers, find out who else your customers know that might want a similar product.

That is just one example. Extending can take many forms. It can be as straight forward as the above example or more esoteric. A successful extension can include a myriad of things like:

- Customer testimonials
- Internal introductions (coworkers, managers and executives)
- External introductions (other groups, departments, institutions, companies or organizations)
- Referrals
- Commitment to try a new product or service
- Teaming or partnership arrangements
- Joint ventures

DO IT AGAIN

In the 1993 hit comedy *Groundhog Day*, Phil Connors (the character played by Bill Murray) finds himself in a time loop, repeating the same day over and over until finally, he is able to break out. Remember, extend does not mean the SALEs Process is finished. On the contrary, if you play your cards correctly, a successful extension just opens the door to start surveying again, this time hopefully with bigger and brighter opportunities.

Just as this chapter outlined a powerful new strategic tool, the SALEs Process, the next chapter will provide you with the skills necessary to ask the best questions and organize your information into useful account profiles and customer databases to really keep things moving in the right direction.

CHAPTER 9

DEVELOPING WINNING STRATEGIES

"I have always thought the actions of men the best interpreters of their thoughts." - John Locke

In putting this chapter together, I spent considerably more time looking for the best introductory quotation that I could find because this is undoubtedly the most valuable information contained within the entire book. The ability to understand actions, both of yourself and of others, and then to use that understanding to attain of your goals, is essential to success in any field, not just in healthcare sales. I applaud Mr. Locke for the clarity of his words and agree with them wholeheartedly.

This chapter is the essence of Pyrametrics. It's all about the "why" and making sense of your customers, especially in situations where their words and actions don't jive. It introduces you to the necessity of building mental databases so you'll be able to find logic in chaos and accurately predict, then drive customer behavior. And finally, it will give you the confidence to take control in a profession where much of your success is dependent on the actions of others.

UNDERSTANDING THE IDIOSYNCRASIES OF YOUR HEALTHCARE CUSTOMERS

Perhaps I'm biased, but while I know that every sector has its own idiosyncrasies and peculiarities, my feeling is that healthcare has more than its share of both. In the past thirty years I have worked in government, technology and healthcare, and in a variety of roles, and I can say with assurance that of the three, your healthcare customers will demonstrate some of the most erratic decision making imaginable. Up to this point, the focus of this book has been on providing you with extensive background information and tools that you can use in preparation for calling on the industry. In the SALEs Process, this equates to your Survey. Now we're shifting to the hard part, learning what to do after you've made first contact.

When clients ask me what I mean when I say that decision making in the healthcare industry can be erratic, I recall this story. One day I was having a conversation with a colleague and he told me, "I'm not going to prescribe anything for my patients that's advertised on TV." Now imagine if you were a rep calling on this guy. What would you make of that statement? At first you'd probably think it was absurd. And in fact it was, especially for a cardiologist. After all, some very important medications are advertised on television - medicines like aspirin which are absolutely essential in cardiac care and others that treat high blood pressure, cholesterol and prevent blood clots. In fact, it would be malpractice not to use them, regardless of whether or not they're advertised.

But, while his comment may have seemed silly to you, I assure you that it didn't to him. In fact, you really don't have to spend too much time in healthcare to hear a lot of this. These are some of the biggest hurdles you're going to have to jump when calling in this industry. And it's not just for pharmaceuticals; every sector will have similar issues. The only way you'll be able to counter this behavior is to understand where it comes from.

Consider this, from the first day of training providers are taught to focus on one thing: patient care. They receive little, if any teaching about business, whether that is management, marketing, finance or sales. While that's optimal for a medical education, it is also somewhat naive when it comes to the real world. After all, healthcare is not dispensed in a vacuum. It is a part of a very complex economy with principles that need mastering as well. In fact, not only is there scant business training, there are also some deep biases against business that get passed on as well.

When I was practicing, I routinely participated in management meetings at both the hospital and medical group level. It was amazing how differently medical and business people think. Here is a good example. One time during a Monday morning partners' meeting I asked the membership, "What is the primary function of our group?" That was a particularly relevant question because of the significant upheaval in the industry at the time. The unanimous answer: "To take care of patients." To which I then replied, "That's wrong. The primary function of our group is to stay in practice because if we're not here no one gets cared for." Survival is the primary goal of any business, medical or otherwise. Customer service (in this case patient care) is but a means to achieve that goal.

Now consider this question: What is the primary function of your sales force? I suspect you'll answer something like, to attract and retain customers, up-sell them where appropriate, and continually increase the revenues obtained from them. In other words, you want to foster long term relationships, develop "sticky" customers and make lots of money. If you answered something like that then I agree with you. Unfortunately, while developing sticky customers may be appropriate in your business, it doesn't translate well into medicine. In fact, no provider or hospital is going to promote the development of "sticky" patients. Neither are they going to publicly profess to making lots of money or even trying to do so. After all, the healthcare industry gets excoriated every time money making or profits are discussed. That's not a political statement. It's just the way it is. And when it comes to fostering long term relationships, there are some differing perspectives on that, too.

Think about what the primary goal of healthcare is, to eradicate disease. Therefore, if a patient comes in sick and I make him better, then I have done my job. As a physician I took great pride in telling my patients, "You're fine. You don't have to come back in anymore." Think about your last visit to the doctor. What would have made you happier, having to come back each week for more therapy, or being sent home with a clean bill of health? As an industry, healthcare's ultimate goal is to cure patients so they don't have to come back. In fact, it's probably the only industry where it's considered a success to NOT have repeat customers.

During my decade in practice, many of the things I did in my earlier years were obsolete by the time I got older. In fact, some of the more lucrative tests and procedures that I did were either sharply curtailed or eliminated completely. We were doing our job so well that we were essentially making ourselves obsolete. From a patient standpoint, this was great. But when you consider it from a business perspective it was horrible.

Imagine what would happen if you told your sales manager, "Hey Frank, I did my job so well that my customers don't ever need to see me again." That would probably not go over very well. After all, you're expected to grow the business, not dry it up. Your priorities, your mindset, your whole way of looking at business are of a certain perspective. Unfortunately, your healthcare customers see things differently. Every time they start to think about up-selling patients, growing the business and expanding revenues, they have to reconcile those thoughts against what's ethical for patient care. Therein lies the fundamental conflict for many of the customers you'll be calling on. It's also the basis for a lot of seemingly incongruous behavior. Now you can see how there might be a disconnect when providers talk with sales people.

So now when you consider my colleague above, his comment makes more sense. He looked at advertising as a shameless attempt to influence behavior that could somehow be detrimental to patient care instead of seeing it like you would– as an attempt to build brand awareness and recognition while trying to maintain existing customers and attract new ones.

With the exception of administrators and a few clinical executives, most of the folks you'll encounter in healthcare are not trained in business. In fact, they are probably some of the least business savvy customers out there. Worse still, they see the world completely different than you do and they may harbor negative feelings toward you simply because of the work you do. Unfortunately too, many are deeply involved in the management and operations of hospitals and groups and this can make the hard job of selling even harder. These are just some of the idiosyncrasies of the customers you've chosen to serve. But at least now you can start to prepare for them.

UNDERSTANDING CUSTOMER BEHAVIOR - THE BASICS

Selling is all about observing, understanding and using that knowledge to drive customer behavior. When customers say what they'll do and then do what they say, the job is easy. It's when they don't, when the words and the actions don't mesh, that you really have to work hard to earn your money. This can be particularly frustrating when you're trying to obtain commitments or get answers to important questions. When it comes to understanding why there can be such a disconnect between what is said and what is done, here are six reasons to explain most of them.

1. They don't know the answer at the time. Sometimes you'll ask a question and the customer won't know the answer. Unfortunately, they may not tell you that. Remember who you're dealing with. Healthcare people don't like being ignorant or worse, being *perceived* as not knowing something. It goes against their training, their psyche and it's very uncomfortable. So instead, they'll either take an educated guess or just make something up only to find out later they can't follow through. These situations can be tough for you to overcome. The key is to recognize a history of these actions early so you're better able to predict them in the future.

2. It's the right answer then. Things change through no fault of yours or the customer's. What might be correct now will be wrong later. Many times I've received commitments from customers only to have things change in a few months. It's difficult to plan for this and it can be even harder to accept, particularly if you have a lot riding on the commitment. But these things happen sometimes. In cases like this you just have to get up, dust yourself off and get back to work.

3. They want you to think they have more power than they really do. Yes, this does happen. Many folks in healthcare are egotistical. They either think of themselves as more important than they really are or want you to think so. Either way, this is a difficult situation because you're expecting, and even counting on something the customer may not be able to deliver. And it can be even harder questioning them about it. Your best bet is to devise a work-around scenario that lets your customer save face while you still move the sales process forward. But this can take time. It's also another reason why you really need to get to know your customers well.

4. They tell you what they think you want to hear. Sometimes customers are just trying to be nice. They are, after all, in the caring business. They may think by exaggerating a little that you will be happy. They want to be your friend, support your cause or get a charge out of helping you. Unfortunately, when it comes time to collect they can't or don't deliver. You really can't fault their intentions, but it can be very frustrating nonetheless. Your only option here is to try and set better expectations on the front end.

5. They want to get rid of you. Some folks just don't like sales people and they will tell you (politely, or not) whatever they think will get you out the door the fastest. Others may like you just fine but can't bear to give you bad news, so they embellish a little and hope you'll go away. There's not a lot you can do in either case except to try and recognize it up front and move on. Then make sure you don't let it happen again. This speaks to the value of maintaining sound mental databases on your customers (a topic we'll take up shortly). Remember the old saying - *Fool me once shame on you. Fool me twice, shame on me.* Always keep track of these customer types so they don't fool you twice.

6. They want to mess with you. It happens, so don't think it doesn't. There are malicious people everywhere and at times they'll see you as a soft target and let you have it. In cases like this, always retain your composure and your self respect. Then decide how to carry on from there. Remember, there are some customers who are just not worth the hassle, regardless of what they can do for your quota. These are the ones you need to avoid like the plague.

CUSTOMER BEHAVIOR - DECODED

It can be quite frustrating, especially when you're counting so heavily on someone to follow through with their commitment, only to see it fall apart. That's why it's so important to be able to understand, and then predict customer behavior accurately. As a cardiologist I would experience this all the time. For instance, patients would swear to me they've been taking their medications religiously not knowing that I just received a call from the pharmacy reporting they never even picked up the prescription. Or they would come in saying they quit smoking only to have cigarettes fall out their pocket during the examination. Those were some of the more glaring examples, but there were many others as well.

Fortunately for me, the consequences of this type of behavior fell on the patient. After all, we were dealing with *their* health. If they didn't care about it, there wasn't much I could do. This is not the case in sales however. In a sales situation when I ask a question or seek a commitment, I'm personally dependent upon the customer's response and ultimately their follow through. Unfortunately then, if they're saying one thing and doing another, it's up to me to try and make sense of it because my future depends on it. At the end of the day, if I don't know how to predict, or at least interpret customer behavior, and then be able to devise a work-around, my success is in jeopardy. What I found is that if you want to decode customer behavior accurately then you first need to commit yourself to the task. Once you've done that, Pyrametrics is there to help.

Recall the three fundamental principles of Pyrametrics:

1. Anything complex can be made easier if it is first broken down into its component parts.

When it comes to understanding customer behavior, I always found it much more efficient to try and determine their basic drivers and then go from there. After all, as complex as we all are, at the end of the day we really only do things for a few basic reasons. When it comes to your healthcare customers, I think you'll find what drives you, drives them; with a few exceptions. The more you train yourself to look for these, the better off you'll be in the long run. Remember, with knowledge comes power. And with that power comes the ability to predict customer behavior (or at least to understand it). Then you're really doing well. Some of those drivers are:

- For patient care - When it comes to healthcare, the overriding concern for most is making things better for the patient. When looking for drivers of customer behavior, start here first.
- For money - Whenever someone says it's not about the money, it's always about the money!

Many of the more contentious arguments we had as a group were about money. You'd think with a bunch of well-paid cardiologists that wouldn't matter so much but it still did. Money is a very touchy subject for physicians and healthcare providers in general, particularly with the current environment. Nevertheless, there is still a stigma associated with being perceived as too financially focused. After all, the focus is supposed to be on patient care, not making a buck. And as we discussed above, things can run counter to each other. That said, I still never met a physician who didn't aggressively protect his share. But the whole issue still puts providers in a bind. Speak too loudly about money and you look greedy and uncaring, don't speak enough and you might lose some of it. Either way, it's in your best interest to know this exists.

- For power - Everyone likes power. And for providers one of the most basic powers is controlling their own destiny, doing things their way and staying independent. This is why many went into the field in the first place and is especially relevant in the current climate. Therefore, as a sales rep calling on these folks always keep this in mind.
- For advancement - This may not be as big a deal as some of the other drivers because the medical field really does not offer a significant career advancement pathway. Unlike the corporate world where a mail room clerk can rise to be CEO some day, that doesn't usually happen in medicine. For most, the things they do on their first day will be exactly the same as what they do on their last.
- For recognition - Browse the internet sometime and look at all the sites for Top Doctors or America's Best Specialists, etc. Then look at the various physicians grading websites. A lot depends on perception. In fact, some new payment models are weighing this very highly. Everyone wants to be recognized and your healthcare customers are no different. This can be especially prevalent in the academic and research worlds too, but for slightly different reasons. In their world publishing articles, completing projects and landing big grants is paramount. It's all about recognition there as well. As you get to know your customers, these folks will be easy to spot.
- Because it makes them feel good - We all do things because it makes us feel good. At the end of the day, this is a pretty big driver too.
- For revenge - Oh yes, this happens. Egos are big in healthcare and sometimes they get bruised. When that happens there can be hell to pay for the transgressor. Never discount revenge as a driver for customer behavior.

2. When trying to understand something, move from the general to the specific.

When it comes to customer behavior everyone is a little different. The key then is to try and find some characteristics that are applicable to everyone and then use that as a base which can then be applied to your individual customers. The first of these characteristics is:

Everything We Do is For a Reason.

This concept was touched on briefly in the last chapter but it's here where we really drill down to the bedrock. Recall that Pyrametrics is all about changing your perspective so you understand why things happen and not just that they do happen. Therefore, when considering customer behavior remember, don't make false assumptions. Everything is done for a reason. Train yourself to find that reason!

For example, one of the frustrations I found in working with a large medical group was the difficulty in making decisions. Decision making in the healthcare space, particularly among providers, can be problematic everywhere and that applies whether you're a partner trying to run the practice or a sales rep trying to sell into it. Many issues, even the most mundane, are hashed and rehashed before finally being resolved. This is just the way providers are. The reason is because they are analytical by training, conservative by nature and used to having their opinions heard. They also do not want to make mistakes by rushing into a decision. In patient care there is no such thing as too much information because missing something, even a small tidbit can make the difference between life and death. Consequently, decision making can be a very lengthy and demanding process. If you're in a sales situation with a group of providers and it seems to be stalled, this might be the reason why. Now you can begin to apply a general characteristic to your individual sales situations.

The second characteristic is:

When Faced with Similar Circumstances, People Do Similar Things.

We are all creatures of habit and the older we get, the more habitual we become. This is true for everybody, not just healthcare customers. Think about what you do when you're stressed. You may be stressed for any one of a million reasons, but regardless of the reason, you probably still react the same way. For instance in my case, when I am stressed I tend to want to go for run. I find that it clears my mind, tires me out and the endorphin rush makes me forget what I was worried about, if only for a little bit. I'm sure you have your own routine.

The same kind of behavior can apply to groups and organizations, large and small. When I was in practice, one of the things that continuously vexed me was the rigidity in decision making. We would keep responding to the same situations, over and over again, in the exact same way as before because that was the way it was always done. It was rare, if ever, that we responded to a situation proactively rather than reactively. And I can't remember a time when we really thought outside the box and came up with something unique. This wasn't just limited to our group though. Some of the hospitals that I worked in repeatedly responded to the same situations by doing the exact same things too. Whether it dealt with staffing, treatment protocols, physician issues, you name it, every decision was pretty much the same.

If you're wondering why this is, the likely reason is because healthcare workers are trained from the beginning to stick with treatments that work. After all, while creativity and free thinking might work well at Apple or Microsoft, they are not always the best for patient care. For example, if you came into the ER having a heart attack, I'm sure you wouldn't appreciate your doctor saying, "OK Mrs. Jones, I know an angioplasty would work well here, but let's try an enema and see what that does."

As you start to call on different accounts, begin to take mental notes about how both the individuals and the organization respond to different situations. I'm sure you'll find that their actions will repeat and be predictable. Once you gain an understanding of how things are done, then it's almost like having a crystal ball you can use to predict future behavior.

Here's another interesting one you should be aware of:

"Groupthink", is Alive and Well in Healthcare.

Wikipedia explains Groupthink as, *"a psychological phenomenon that occurs within a group of people, in which the desire for harmony or conformity in the group results in an incorrect or deviant decision making outcome. Group members try to minimize conflict and reach a consensus decision without critical evaluation of alternative ideas or viewpoints. Loyalty to the group requires individuals to avoid raising controversial issues or alternative solutions"*. When it comes to understanding your healthcare customers, this is 100% spot on accurate and it happens all the time.

When I was in practice, there were countless examples of a handful of folks who dictated the behavior of an entire group. The reason this happened was because while one or two guys took the time to research an issue, the rest didn't. Then they would just go along with whatever else was said because it was so much easier and it avoided conflict. Unfortunately, many times the one or two guys didn't have the right information and so the group would repeatedly make poor decisions and reinforce bad ideas.

That action wasn't limited to just group operations. It happened in the hospital setting too. Rumors would get started and then propagate throughout the community without anyone ever bothering to check the facts or really set the record straight. After a while the rumors we so well spread that everyone just accepted them as truth. I remember many times trying to call BS on things only to get shot down because what I was saying deviated from the group. It was a very interesting, if not frustrating, phenomenon.

If you're in the process of selling something to a healthcare customer and you keep getting stonewalled by erroneous or unusual objections, it may be because of Groupthink in action, particularly if you have just been calling on a few people within the organization. This kind of thing does happen a lot and it only reinforces the need to always sell through an organization, calling on as many folks as you can and repeating your message as often as you can.

Finally, consider this:

Passive Aggressive Behavior is the Rule, Not the Exception.

While there are some aggressive and confrontational types in healthcare, most of the folks you'll deal with are nonconfrontational. By that I mean they don't like forceful or aggressive interaction. If you're wondering why that is, it's because in order to survive medical training you have to know how to play the game and deal with the myriad of inflated egos and overblown personalities endemic to the profession. In short, you don't want to piss anyone off. Then once you get into practice, you don't want to alienate a potential referral source or irritate your partners to the point they won't cover for you. And that's not easy to do particularly because disagreements come about all the time. Unfortunately, because lots of providers take that kind of stuff so personally, it's almost like you're walking on egg shells all the time.

Therefore, when dealing with sales people, many providers will just treat you like everyone else. They'll tell you the most politically correct or least controversial answer and leave it at that. Then they'll just go off and do whatever they want behind your back. In other words, they'll be very passive-aggressive. If you don't believe another word in this book, believe that. I lived it for twenty years. It's true.

For me, that was one of the most troubling things to accept and deal with because I've always been of the mind that if you have an issue with someone or if there's something that needs to be done, it's best to just go straight after it and get it resolved. Unfortunately, things just weren't done that way and it took me while to figure it out. I suspect that it may not be the way you're used to doing things either. After all, in sales you don't have the luxury of pussy-footing around. The clock is ticking and you have a quota to make. Then there's your competition, they're certainly not wasting time either. But as we mentioned before, there are many differences in how healthcare folks do things and how sales people do things. My hope is that as you read this, it will help you avoid what took me many painful years to overcome.

3. Develop a process and stick with it.

Just like anything else, if you want to be successful, you need to follow a process. And the more complicated things are, the more important process becomes. Therefore, when it comes to understanding individual behavior, use the following process:

A. Put yourself out there. If you want to get to know someone then you must break the ice. In business, this means you can ask for an introduction from someone else, you can use social media or you can just go right up and say hello. The onus is on you to extend yourself. People by and large, are shy or busy and not really adept at meeting strangers. So, if you've identified a person you like to meet, then get out there and meet them. It all starts there.

B. CHEW on them. In the previous chapter we introduced the idea of CHEWing. CHEW, as you recall, stands for Children, Hobbies, Education & Wife (spouse). Start to ask questions and find common ground. If you look closely enough, you'll find many areas of common ground. Pick a couple to focus on and make the connection. Then don't let up. Keep the relationships going by actively managing your contacts. And remember the 13 Touch Rule, you need to mix up your messages lest they become old and familiar. If you do it right, in time folks will come to appreciate and even expect to hear from you. Then you know you've made a lasting connection.

C. Pay close attention. As you get out and start meeting customers, make sure to pay close attention to what they say and what they do. Look for areas where words and actions jive and don't jive. Then try to figure out why. Look for consistencies in responses and behaviors. Understand the environment and then try to figure out what drives your customers to do the things they do. This can be very difficult because a customer may tell you something one day but then contradict it several weeks later. Remember, it is very hard to stay consistent when you're trying to hide, lie about or cover something up. It is almost a certainty that they will slip up somewhere. This is even true in benign situations where no one is trying to be sneaky. You just need to be paying attention in order to pick up on it.

D. Form a hypothesis and test it. One of the first clients I engaged with after starting Health Comm Strategies was a large manufacturer on the East Coast. They had reached out to me to help them market and sell a product for the cardiology space. As part of my business development efforts I established relationships with their director of sales and representatives from their training section. We had established a great dialogue and everything seemed to be going well.

But then just as quickly the process stalled. We were still having a dialogue but a firm commitment was not being reached. I began to seriously wonder why. As I surveyed their company further, I found out that the decision making process required buy-in from three different groups; sales, training and product. The product guys tell the sales guys how they think the items should be marketed. Then the sales guys ask the training guys to help them develop those necessary skills in the sales force and then they go out and sell. As far as I knew, both the sales guys and training guys were excited to bring me on board. If there was a hold up, it was likely coming from product.

Not long after that we had a teleconference scheduled. Including myself, representatives from all three groups were invited. When the time came however, only the sales and training guys attended. No one from product joined the call. Everyone was very apologetic and effusive but it seemed like just a little too much. I suspected they were embarrassed. Even though no one came out and said it, it now looked like product was indeed the hold up. The question now was, why? To answer that I had to form a hypothesis and validate it. Then I could figure out how to overcome it.

One of the reasons the sales and training guys were interested in me was because I had some unique perspectives on the cardiology market and how providers think. Unfortunately though, one of my strongest recommendations ran counter to what the product folks were saying. As a provider I thought their approach was not accurate. It didn't make sense to me. Furthermore, they weren't following Pyrametrics - they were making predictions about specific customer behavior BEFORE understanding what really drives it. Since it was their job to design a marketing strategy, this may have caused friction. After all, if they brought me on board only to upend everything they'd been advocating to that point, and it worked, how would that make them look? Or, if they brought me on and it didn't work, they'd probably get hammered for wasting money on a useless endeavor. Either way, if my hypothesis was true, this was a big problem.

Shortly thereafter, I was passing through their area and arranged to meet with the sales director. During that meeting I asked how things were progressing.

"Well Mark", he said, "We still have some internal hold ups." That's when I decided to test the hypothesis. Without even blinking I responded, "That's OK. I know my coming on board would put product in a tough spot. They're probably trying to decide if I'm a liability or an asset." Then I sat back and watched for clues but he didn't even flinch. He just smiled and said, "Yeah. They have they're own way of doing things." At that point my hypothesis was verified.

This may seem like an unusual example but customers do this kind of thing all the time. They will change plans, shift gears and do all sorts of things during the sales process. Things that could impact you very significantly. How and if you choose to overcome this is up to you. But what I have found is that leaving unanswered questions out there can be detrimental in the long run. I've also found that if you go in confident, with guns blazing and act as though you already know exactly what's going on then you're far more likely to get a good response than if you sheepishly tried to ask a few questions.

People respond to confidence and deliberate behavior. So act as though you already know what going on. That way if your hypothesis is correct, then you know straight up. If not, either they will correct you outright or they will at least flash a few facial gestures that will tell you you're going in the wrong direction. Then you can rework your hypothesis and try again later. Remember, in this life you have to go after what you want and that is especially true in sales. No one is out there spoon-feeding you. Be aggressive, creative and persistent. If things don't pan out the first time, keep at it. Eventually they will.

BUILDING YOUR MENTAL DATABASE - GOING BEYOND THE CRM

Once again I'll use an example from clinical medicine to try and introduce an important point.

Fifty years ago if you made it into the hospital with a heart attack, your chance of dying was about 50/50, a coin flip essentially. Over the following two decades or so many straight forward, relatively low cost advances were made in cardiac care that brought the mortality rate down substantially. Things like giving aspirin, oxygen, creating specialized intensive care units and training personnel more deliberately. So good were these interventions, in fact, that the mortality rate was cut to almost 10%. That was a pretty good start but the advances didn't end there.

In the following decades new equipment for diagnosis and treatment, like catheters and stents, and powerful new medications came on line that pushed the mortality rate down even further into the 5-6% range, about where they are today. Unfortunately though, the cost of driving down this mortality from 10% to 5% was much greater than it was to drive it down from 50% to 10%. And today, as we seek to drive the mortality rates down even lower with new molecular and genetic therapies, the cost rises exponentially higher. Therefore, the lower we go with mortality improvement, the more it costs.

Interestingly, a similar phenomenon is occurring in the world of healthcare sales. What started as only selling features and benefits matured rapidly into selling solutions and is now advancing with full force toward trusted advisorship. As problems become more complex, so do the solutions. Unfortunately, so too does the sales cycle and the demand for competent, qualified and highly specialized sales forces. Customers are looking for partners, not vendors. That means you need to understand the customer almost as well as they understand themselves, sometimes even better. And that ain't cheap.

Fielding a sales force today is not a low cost proposition. Not if you want an effective one. Technology like Customer Relationship Management (CRM) programs help to organize information and manage accounts but they can't do it all. Furthermore, tools like these are becoming so popular that not using one is the exception to the rule. In fact, your company probably has one too. The problem is that for most sectors within healthcare there is parity. Everyone is working hard. Everyone is sharp, well trained and motivated. This is the reality whether you're in technology, pharmaceuticals, financial products, software, telecom, instruments, you name it. In other words, your competition is doing the same things you are. So how do you get ahead?

Similar to the clinical example above, if you want to get ahead in healthcare sales today then you need to work smarter and realize that big advancements aren't coming. The low hanging fruit has already been picked. And just like with heart care, you're going to realize that even modest advancements will be expensive. But that's OK, because if you only get small improvements when they're integrated over a large sales force the benefits can still be substantial. The secret is to win the battle in the trenches by mastering the fundamentals better than your competition. Pyrametrics is all about mastering those fundamentals.

Those fundamentals include differentiating yourself favorably at the outset and really knowing your customers. Part of knowing your customers includes what we've presented to this point and also how you maintain and use that knowledge. Having an effective customer database is an essential component of any sales reps armamentarium. Unfortunately, there really is no standard format. You're free to design and manage yours however you want. Just make sure that it contains ALL the important information and that it's in a format you can use.

When I sold for HP, I called on major accounts primarily. As such, I really didn't have that many different customers to remember. So I kept most of their information in my head. Then, as they became better known to me and we became friends, it was easy to keep everyone straight. When I jumped into clinical medicine all my customers were patients, and there were thousands of them. There was no way I could keep all that information in my head even if I wanted to. Fortunately we had medical records, paper first, then electronic. Your situation will be somewhere in the middle of those two extremes. Remember though, in medicine as in sales, you can never know too much about your customers.

NOW WHAT?

Throughout this book we have identified a process and attempted to follow it. If your goal is to sell successfully into one of the most challenging and complex but lucrative industries in the world, you need to be prepared. You need to identify what your goals are, then create a plan to attain them. You need to research, prepare and dig deeper than your competition. Then you need to execute. And as you execute, you need to learn about your customers, understand their behavior, overcome their objections and take control. You need to keep moving forward, day by day, one step at a time, until you're finished. Then in the end, you can claim what is yours. After that you get to line up and do it again.

Welcome to the world of healthcare sales!

In our final chapter we'll introduce some concepts to help take you over the top, to recognize the biggest hurdles in healthcare sales and how you can overcome them. Then we'll give you a call to action. Because from there on out, the rest is up to you.

CHAPTER 10

SUCCEEDING AT SUCCESS

"Inaction breeds doubt and fear. Action breeds confidence and courage. If you want to conquer fear, do not sit at home and think about it. Go out and get busy." - Dale Carnegie

While there are many people who fail to succeed, there are significantly more who succeed at failing. Although this may seem like a simple play on words, I assure you it isn't. After all, it's okay to be in the first group. Success can be elusive, even to those with exceptional skills. But I can't imagine anyone wanting to be in the second group. In the last chapter we discussed strategies for success. In this final chapter we'll present strategies to avoid failure.

When it comes to failure, the overriding cause is usually fear. For some, fear can be a great motivator, but for others it can paralyze them. While everyone is fearful of something, successful people refuse to let it stand in their way. If you're going to be calling in the healthcare industry, you'll need to harness your fears and reservations in order to succeed. Remember, how you choose to address your fears is not only a big predictor of how far you'll go in sales, but also in life.

TAKING THE FEAR OUT OF HEALTHCARE SALES

There are a lot of frightening things in sales, and healthcare sales are certainly no different. In preparing for this writing I surveyed hundreds of sales people to try and find out what they considered to be their greatest fears when calling on this industry. What follows are their top five answers and my strategies to help you overcome them. Interestingly, the answers provide a very good review of everything we've covered to this point.

The Fourth Runner Up: Not being taken seriously by my healthcare customers.

We have discussed this off and on throughout the previous chapters, but it bears repeating once again. Calling on healthcare customers can be very intimidating, especially since many are highly educated, very prominent in their field and can be less receptive to the sales process or the people who engage in it. They are also very busy and can be difficult to meet with. If you want to be successful, you need to be persistent. Your goal is always to add value to the patient care process and to be seen as a valuable resource and indispensable member of the healthcare team. If you do that consistently, you will be taken seriously.

Whether or not you're able to do that depends on you to adopt the proper mindset. After all, before anyone will exhibit confidence in you, you must first possess confidence in yourself. Remember, you alone determine how others treat you. Never forget that your confidence, your attitude and your demeanor all make a big difference when you engage with others. Never allow anyone to treat you disrespectfully or unprofessionally. And never adopt a submissive of deferential attitude. You'll only be hurting your chances if you do. Your customers are used to dealing with sharp and competent individuals. Make sure you're one of them.

Also remember that no one is as smart as you may think they are. Your healthcare customers may know a lot about patient care, but you are the expert in what you sell. And no one knows what you know better than you do. After all, every patient is treated in one of three ways; medically, surgically or with reassurance. Therefore, without your products and services, most providers could only talk to their patients. That makes you a very valuable resource and that's something you should never forget.

The Third Runner Up: Not knowing what I should be doing in the healthcare account.

Healthcare accounts are no different than accounts in any other field when it comes to knowing what to do. If you are going be successful then you better have set goals, a plan for attaining those goals and you'd better not waste time. After all, in sales time is a very valuable commodity and there are stiff penalties for squandering it. You have only so much time to make your quota and only so much time to engage with customers. Therefore, you constantly need to be weighing what you're doing against what you could have done.

For sales reps this is an amazingly easy calculation and one that I encourage you to pursue. It starts with the realization that in selling everything comes down to making your quota and that if you're not doing things to advance that cause then you are wasting both time and money. Consider this example:

Your 2012 Quota	$	20,000,000
Working days in 2012 (estimate)		250
Your daily 2012 Quota	$	80,000
Your hourly 2012 Quota (9am to 4pm)	$	13,334
Your 2012 Quota per Working Minute	$	222

Therefore, in order to stay on target, each minute you should be selling $222. That is how much your time is worth. Now, consider the costs associated with performing tasks other than selling:

Chat with your buddy (15 minutes)	$	3,333
Social media (30 minutes)	$	6,660
Meeting (45 minutes)	$	9,990
Dentist (90 minutes)	$	19,998

This table is Pyrametrics at its finest. And it helps you to keep your eye on the ball by recognizing that everything you do must bring you closer to making your goal. Another way that Pyrametrics helps to keep you on target is with the Process Management Algorithm. This was introduced early on but is being repeated here to remind you of the three things you should be doing at all times.

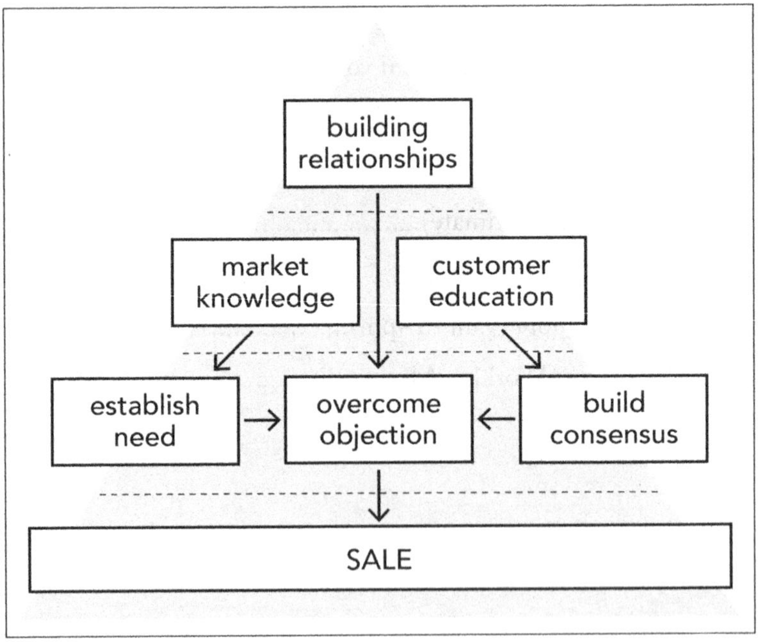

By first determining the value of your time and then focusing only on those things that bring you closer to the sale, you won't have to worry about not knowing what to do.

The Second Runner Up: Not having my customers want to listen to me.

As we've mentioned previously, there is nothing more important than your preparation because there is no second chance to make a good first impression. Your healthcare customers are sharp and demanding, and they will know instantly whether or not you're adding value to their day. With that in mind, consider these two introductions. Both are real world examples from my time in medicine. I only changed the names. When I was practicing, I experienced far too many of the first and not nearly enough of the second.

1. "Hi, my name is Joe and I'm with HCS. I was wondering if I could have a little bit of your time so that you could tell me what you do here?"

2. "Greetings, Dr. Moronell. My name is Joe Salesguy and I'm with Health Comm Strategies. I believe that we can help you get more efficiency out of your existing EMR system, particularly in regard to data mining and risk profiles. Would you be available to discuss these issues for thirty minutes on Wednesday morning?"

Now, let's analyze not just what was actually said, but the underlying message received.

The first approach immediately gets off on the wrong foot by focusing on the rep, not the customer. "I was wondering", sounds a bit flippant, so too does introducing his company just by stating the initials. Unless he works for IBM, or an equally famous outfit, he should not be so causal. He was also too informal with just offering his first name.

Furthermore, as the customer I don't really care what a rep was wondering. Nor do I want to do his job for him and that is exactly what it sounds like he's asking me to do. The approach seems arrogant. The rep should have prepared for the call before we met so that he has an idea of what I do and does not need me to waste my time telling him. It gets worse from there. In asking for a meeting, "A little bit," is vague, undefined and doesn't tell me what to expect or how much time I need to set aside for the meeting. Healthcare providers are used to dealing in exact figures: The heart artery is 99 percent occluded. Her temperature is 101.5 degrees Fahrenheit. His blood pressure is 120/70 mm Hg. When we see patients, we are also used to dealing in very specific blocks of time and I worked very hard to stay on schedule. Sales reps who were unable to afford me the same courtesy and consideration weren't calling on me for long and I guarantee that the rest of the industry felt the same way.

Now let's review the second approach. It begins with a formal introduction followed by a powerful opening statement regarding a very relevant issue. This tells me the rep has done his homework. He knows about my problems and he has a possible solution. Finally, he understands my schedule and is adapting to it by being specific about when, how much time is needed and the agenda for the meeting. And if Wednesday afternoon doesn't work for me, I have all the information I need to suggest an alternate time.

Consider the two approaches. Which rep do you think is going to get a meeting? Equally important, which rep is starting out on an equal footing with the customer? Which rep is adding value and laying the foundation for a long-term business relationship? Healthcare customers want to buy from people they know, like and trust not to waste their time. And in that way they are no different from any other customers. If you are going to be successful, you'd better add value at all times. Remember, just as there are opportunity costs for the things you chose to do, there are similar costs for your customers. But if you always focus on adding value for your customers, you won't have to worry about them not wanting to listen to you.

The First Runner Up: Not having my message resonate with the customer.

Your messages need to focus on what the customer wants to hear, not on what you want to say. After all, your customers don't care about you. They only care what you can do for them and their patients. This is the mindset change you need to make if you haven't already.

For some reps, this can be a very difficult transition. In the end, it all comes down to the content of your messages. You must be contributing something that is relevant. Remember, in the course of their day, your healthcare customers are bombarded with demands on their time and attention. They learn very quickly what is relevant and what is just noise. In order for your messages to rise above the din and get heard, you need to ensure they pertain to something very important. That is how you'll resonate with your customers

Pyrametrics teaches that you begin with the general and move to the specific. For example then, when it comes to the healthcare industry there are three issues that are central to almost every buying decision your customers engage in. They are:

- Declining reimbursements.
- Increased competition.

And if you are a medical group, then maintaining your independence is paramount. Or if you are with a hospital system, then attracting and retaining providers, payers and patients is critical for your survival.

If you begin each interaction with a message that addresses one of these critical topics, you'll be much more likely to get their attention. From that point on, whether or not you continue to resonate depends on you. That is why you must carefully prepare for each encounter. In much the same way that an attorney guides the witness along with targeted questioning, so too must you guide the customer to the sale.

Teach yourself to think through each engagement BEFORE it occurs. Have primary and secondary goals that you want to accomplish with each meeting. If you sense things are deviating from your course, try and regroup and stay on target. Otherwise, move to your back up goals and see those through. Feel free to support your messages with collaterals too. An effective collateral program can go a long way in helping you resonate with your customers.

The Winner & Biggest Healthcare Sales Fear: Making sure that I don't miss opportunities.

Healthcare accounts can be complex and challenging. As such, many reps today try and limit their calls to only those things they are the most familiar with. Or, they focus all their energies on one particular customer type without branching out further into the account. It's no wonder then that many are not successful. Successfully selling into the healthcare sector today means selling through the entire organization.

Selling through the organization means that you're selling to everyone. If you are selling HIT, for example, remember that in today's hospital or medical group HIT is so ingrained in the facility that you cannot discuss any part of their operations without at least considering it. Of course, that can be problematic as well. Now, instead of just calling on one department for a single application, you have to blanket the entire facility. For someone not used to doing this, it can be a stressful proposition.

One of the things I teach clients is to be as analytical and detailed in your preparation and follow through as you can. These accounts are complex and the only way to insure you don't miss anything is to be meticulous in your execution. In the case of selling HIT to a hospital then it might mean you need to construct detailed account profiles including schematic diagrams of the account. Here is an example of one such diagram that was used by a client selling telecom services to a hospital system.

In the following drawing, every arrow represents a possible opportunity to send and receive data. You can see that in order to cover this account completely, there needs to be significant coordination across the entire account. Therefore, if you're used to calling on just the CIO or CTO, it could be very stressful trying to engage with the hospital administrator, the ER director, the head nurse for the OR and all the providers in the different groups and departments. All of a sudden your job just got a whole lot harder since talking with these new customer types requires a different focus and plan of attack. But it's something you're going to have to do if you want to succeed.

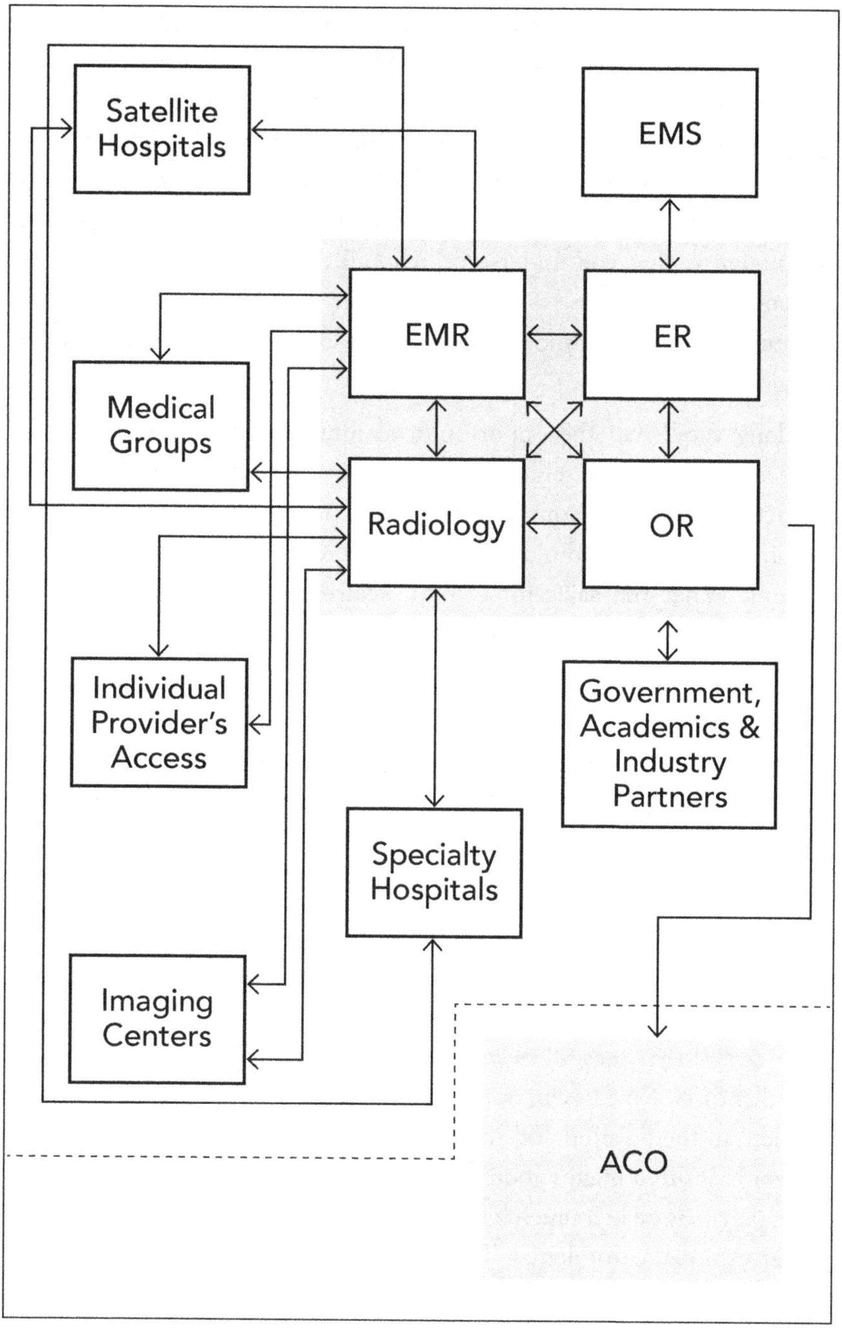
Satellite Hospitals
EMS
EMR
ER
Medical Groups
Radiology
OR
Individual Provider's Access
Government, Academics & Industry Partners
Specialty Hospitals
Imaging Centers
ACO

Another case of being meticulous and methodical when it comes to healthcare sales can be found in the world of pharmaceuticals. I refer to this as *Understanding the Disease Treatment Process*. In my experience I have found few reps that were willing to really broaden their understanding and go the extra mile. Now, this does not mean that as a rep you are trying to become pseudo-physicians and develop expertise in specific therapies. What it does mean though is that you understand who all the different players are in the treatment of certain diseases so that you can expand your contacts develop opportunities beyond the most obvious targets. One such example is pertinent to the world of cardiology.

Not long ago I had the opportunity to interact with the sales force of a pharmaceutical company selling a specific drug for the treatment of chest pain and heart attack. Because of the nature of the drug it was being sold primarily to the interventional cardiologists; those who do the angioplasties and stent placement. What the sales force didn't realize was that depending on the dynamics of the particular hospital and the community, many other physicians may actually have had the opportunity to begin the drug as well.

In a large hospital that I am very familiar with, heart patients can be referred in from many different locations including outlying hospitals and clinics, primary care offices, other specialists' offices and emergency rooms. Depending upon from where they initially present it may be quite appropriate to begin that particular medication there and not wait until the patient is actually seen by the interventional cardiologist.

Also, depending on how the group is structured the interventional cardiologist my not even be the first cardiologist to see the patient. In some groups the general cardiologist sees all new patients and then calls the interventionalist later. Other discrepancies can occur at discharge. It may be that one doctor sees the patient in the hospital and someone else sees them after they go home. In other words, it often makes good sense to sell the drug to these other providers because they may be in a much better position to prescribe the medication than the interventional cardiologist. That is why it is so important for the reps to not only know what the drug does, but also who could potentially prescribe it and how the specific treatment community is set up to manage the particular diseases their drugs treat.

Acquiring knowledge like this is not always easy but it can be very beneficial for those who are willing to make the effort. When faced with these kinds of challenges, keep Pyrametrics in mind and use the skills you've obtained to prepare and execute properly. Remember, at the end of the day, success depends on going further than your competition. In today's market everyone is working hard and trying to get that edge. But healthcare is still relatively wide open because until now, most reps have been content just calling on a few familiar faces. You have the chance to make significant progress if you're willing to step outside your comfort zone and dig deeper than you ever have before. If you are deliberate in your preparation and methodical in your execution, you will not miss opportunities.

FINAL THOUGHTS

Calling on healthcare customers is challenging. Your customers are a unique and demanding breed, and your success will be determined by how well you can establish relationships with them. But establishing those relationships takes time. There is only one sure way to succeed in sales and that is by being persistent.

Clearly, all of the information put forward in this book will take time to master. You will not become proficient overnight. But that's okay. Take the time to implement your new skills slowly, moving from customer to customer, account to account, deliberately and in a manner you feel comfortable with. Pyrametrics works. The tools presented herein were designed only after years in the industry and with perspectives from both sides of the table. Now it's up to you. Don't be afraid to take this information and modify it to meet your specific needs. Be creative in your execution. And if one way doesn't work, keep trying, because there is a good chance the next one will.

Good luck and good selling.

EPILOGUE

MOVING FORWARD

"It always seems impossible until it's done." - Nelson Mandela

WANT TO REALLY REV UP YOUR HEALTHCARE SALES FORCE AND WIN MORE BUSINESS?

1. Is your sales force exceeding expectations or is there room for improvement?

2. Do you have to call on new customer types that you are unfamiliar with or intimidated by?

3. Are you trying to penetrate new areas within the healthcare market but just don't know who to call to get started?

4. Are you introducing a new brand that absolutely cannot afford to fail?

5. Are you in a competitive situation and cannot afford to lose?

If your sales force could benefit from a customized program that will give them the tools to understand their customers, the environment and the key issues pertaining to the healthcare industry as well as providing them with the skills to craft powerful and winning messages, then it's time to call Health Comm Strategies and bring the power of Pyrametrics to you. Our programs are designed to meet the specific needs of your organization and outfit your sales force to move past the competition and win business now and in the future. Here's just a sample of what we can do for you.

Specialized Certification Programs for Pyrametrics

Whether you're in pharmaceuticals, finance, insurance, information technology, telecommunications, hospital/group operations or any other field, let Health Comm Strategies bring the power of Pyrametrics to your sales force with three specialized certification programs designed specifically for your organization and guaranteed to have you master the complex and challenging world of healthcare sales. Our certification programs include:

- Tier I, Intern Level Certification
- Tier II, Resident Level Certification
- Tier III, Specialist Level Certification

Here is our pledge, we are so confident in our Pyrametrics system that if you don't see results, you don't pay. Call Health Comm Strategies and ask about our certification programs now.

Specialized Consulting Services

Let the professionals at Health Comm Strategies help you design, develop and implement state of the art sales and marketing programs to take your organization to the next level. Our service line includes:

Account Strategy

- Account familiarity & understanding
- Account profiling
- Resource allocation

Sales Force Optimization

- Develop relevant strategic selling programs
- Sales force modeling
- Compensation planning
- Synergistic team building

Message Generation & Reinforcement

- Sales call scripting
- Accompaniment on sales call
- Collateral development

Event Planning

- Customer seminars & webinar content
- Trade show messaging & participation

Product Development

- New product conceptualization
- Solution design
- Product roll-outs
- Strategic Partnerships
- Synergistic team building
- Synergistic product development

Other Services

Keynote Speaking

- Alignment of Strategy, Message and Sales Force
- Pyrametrics - Moneyball in the Healthcare Sector
- Into the mind of the HCP
- Strategic Selling into the Healthcare Space
- LEAN Selling

Individual Sales Training

Put the Power of Pyrametrics to work for you as you prepare to jump into healthcare sales. Throughout the training arm, The Cardiac & Technology Sales Training Institute, we'll provide you with powerful and specific sales training that will put you years ahead of your fellow candidates and enable you to land that plum job in healthcare sales. Classes are forming monthly, so call us now.

Resources Available for Your Organization

1. Textbook - *Overview of the Medical Landscape* - A primer for healthcare sales professionals. E-Book available NOW!

2. White Papers/Thought Leadership
    a. LEAN Selling
    b. Applied Pyrametrics for the IT, Telecommunications & Pharma industries.
    c. Strategic Selling into the Healthcare Sector

3. And coming soon - *Applied Pyrametrics - Case Studies for Sales Success.*

Don't forget to check out our websites:

- healthcommstrategies.com
- healthsalestraining.com

Or follow us on social media:

- Facebook: Health Comm Strategies, Cardiac & Technology Sales Training Institute
- LinkedIn Group: Selling Effectively to Healthcare
- Twitter: @HealthCommStrat

APPENDIX

THE PHYSICIAN SPECIALTIES

INTRODUCTION

Although it has been mentioned previously, it still bears repeating. All physicians are not created equal, nor do they practice equally. Understanding the unique characteristics of the various physician specialties is a necessary skill for successful healthcare sales. Also, understanding the specifics of the individual specialty types and how they incorporate technology into their practice models is valuable.

This section lays out the numerous physician specialties in terms of their general classification (medical, surgical, other), training, diseases treated, general office layout, technology requirements and how today's political and economic climates are effecting it.

It is almost guaranteed that as a sales professional, your products and services will be relevant to some, but not all types of physicians. Therefore, having a firm understanding of what your future customers may be looking for is vital for future success. As you have previously read, building a complete customer profile is essential for sales success. Knowing as much as you can about what your customers do, how their offices are arranged, who they serve and what goods and services they need to perform most efficiently will help you to be successful as well. This section was created in part to serve as a reference guide for your future sales activities.

THE MEDICAL SPECIALTIES

In general, physician specialties are classified as medical, surgical or other. They can also be differentiated as to whether they treat adults, children (pediatrics) or both. Medical specialties have their basic roots in internal medicine (adult patients) and pediatrics (child patients) and are classically differentiated from surgical specialties due to their training, philosophy and less intensive reliance on procedures as a method of treatment. Although in today's modern medical environment, many medical specialties perform extensive procedures as well.

Listed below are the most common medical specialties encountered:

- Allergy & Immunology
- Aviation Medicine
- Cardiology
- Endocrinology
- Family Practice
- Gastroenterology
- Geriatrics
- Hematology & Oncology
- Infectious Disease
- Internal Medicine
- Nephrology
- Neurology
- Occupational Health
- Pediatrics

- Pulmonology & Critical Care
- Rehabilitation Medicine
- Rheumatology

1. Allergy & Immunology

Specialty Description: Allergists & Immunologists deal with diseases of the immune system as well as other systems when the immune system is responsible for the affliction. It is a relatively small field and specialists of this kind will be found primarily in larger cities and academic institutions. There are two fundamental areas of study - immunodeficiency (when the immune system is insufficient and/or unable to mount an effective response to a disease) and autoimmunity (where the person's own immune systems attacks the body).

Sub types/related fields: Allergology (the study of allergy and hypersensitivity)

Recognizable Diseases: Asthma, typical & atypical allergies, HIV (AIDS), lupus, rheumatoid arthritis, Hashimoto's (thyroid) disease, myasthenia gravis and transplant rejection being the most common.

Training: Medical school (4 yrs), internal medicine residency (3 yrs), fellowship (1-2 yrs).

Practice type: May be solo or group practice, single or multi-specialty, out-patient primarily.

Technology: EMR, practice management (billing & office management) system, specialty laboratory and blood testing equipment, X-ray machine. If part of a large, multi-specialty practice or group setting, there may be more diagnostic equipment or affiliation with an imaging center.

For more information: http://www.aaaai.org/home.aspx

2. Cardiology

Specialty Description: Cardiologists (cardiovascular disease specialists) deal with diseases of the heart and vascular system. They also treat related illnesses such as hypertension (high blood pressure), hypercholesterolemia (high cholesterol), obesity and related issues. They can treat both adults and children, but it is unusual for someone to do both, except electrophysiologists. Cardiologists are not cardiovascular surgeons and as such they do not perform bypass surgeries, valve repairs, transplants, etc. Cardiovascular surgery is a surgical subspecialty and has a completely different training process. There are also significant differences in the equipment used, where they practice and the size and composition of their respective offices. This is an important point because much of the general population confuses this in everyday communication. As a sales professional, it is important for you to know the differences.

Most cardiologists practice in a group setting with all subtypes being included. As part of the general restructuring of the field of medicine, cardiologists are selling their practices in record numbers and their groups are now becoming part of hospital organizations.

Sub types/related fields: There are several fields within the overall specialty of cardiology - Interventional Cardiology, Invasive, Non-Interventional Cardiology, Non-Invasive Cardiology, and Electrophysiology.

a. Interventional Cardiology - this subset of cardiologists treats disease through the use of invasive testing and procedures such as cardiac catheterization, angioplasty (balloon dilation of arteries), stenting, IVUS (intravascular ultrasound) and other modalities). The majority of their day is spent in the acute or hospital setting although they do have offices.

b. Invasive, Non-Interventional Cardiology - this subset of cardiologists treats disease in a similar manner as interventional cardiologists except they do not perform angioplasty or stent placement. Their primary function is diagnosis of cases such as an acute heart attack (myocardial infarction). Once their job is completed, they will turn over care to the interventionists for continuation of the treatment process.

c. Non-Invasive Cardiology - this subset of cardiologists treats similar types of disease but they generally are not trained in invasive procedures. A new and emerging subspecialty of cardiology includes the imaging specialist who uses new and existing diagnostic technologies such as cardiac MRI (CMR), cardiac CT (CCT), ultrasound (echocardiography) and nuclear medicine for diagnosis and treatment.

d. Electrophysiology - this subset of cardiologists treats diseases of the electrical system of the heart almost exclusively. They are invasive in the sense that many of their procedures do involve entering the body. They perform mainly pacemaker placements, defibrillator placements, ablations and other related activities.

Recognizable Diseases: Myocardial infarction (heart attack)/acute coronary syndromes (ACS), valvular heart disease, vascular disease, congenital heart disease and congestive heart failure.

Training: Medical school (4 yrs), internal medicine or pediatrics residency (3 yrs), fellowship (3-5 yrs).

Practice type: Usually a group setting although solo practitioners still exist. The current medical climate is forcing many groups to merge into bigger groups or sell out and become employed by hospital systems. Cardiologists spend significant time in the hospital but do have office hours as well.

Technology: EMR, practice management system, specialty laboratory and blood testing equipment. May also have/own standalone (or included) imaging centers with some or all of the following equipment:

- Echocardiography (ultrasound)
- Stress testing
- Nuclear medicine
- CT
- CMR (Cardiac MRI)
- Catheterization laboratory
- Ambulatory surgery center

For more information: http://www.cardiosource.org/

3. Endocrinology

Specialty Description: Endocrinologists deal primarily with diseases of the endocrine system (pituitary, thyroid, adrenals, ovaries, testes, and pancreas) and the manner in which hormones are secreted throughout the body. Many diseases can be associated with endocrinology.

Sub types/related fields: Diabetology (diabetes specialist) and fertility specialists.

Recognizable Diseases: Diabetes, hypertension, infertility, adrenal insufficiency, thyroid disorders.

Training: Medical school (4 yrs), internal medicine residency (3 yrs), endocrinology fellowship (2-3 yrs).

Practice type: Office based primarily with both group (small) and solo-practices common. Affiliation with larger hospitals or academic centers is also common.

Technology: EMR, practice management (billing & office management) system, specialty laboratory and blood testing equipment, X-ray machine (possible). If part of a large, multi-specialty practice or group setting there may be more diagnostic equipment or affiliation with an imaging center.

For more information: https://www.aace.com/

4. Family Practice

Specialty Description: Family practitioners deal with general medical issues of adults and children. They are a unique specialty in that their training includes extensive familiarity with both pediatric and adult medicine. They also get training in basic, usually out-patient surgical procedures. Some have training and experience in obstetrics. Their focus is on both the treatment of acute disease, general health and prevention.

Sub types/related fields: Adolescent medicine, geriatrics, sleep medicine and sports medicine.

Recognizable Diseases: The most common illnesses in both adults and children.

Training: Medical school (4 yrs), family practice residency (3 yrs).

Practice type: Office based primarily with both group and solo-practices common.

Technology: EMR, practice management (billing & office management) system, specialty laboratory and blood testing equipment, X-ray machine (possible). If part of a large, multi-specialty practice or group setting there may be more diagnostic equipment or affiliation with an imaging center.

For more information:
http://www.aafp.org/online/en/home.html

5. Gastroenterology

Specialty Description: Gastroenterologists are subspecialists of internal medicine who deal with diseases of the digestive system.

Sub types/related fields: Hepatology (liver diseases), transplant hepatology.

Recognizable diseases: Ulcers, hepatitis, Crohn's Disease, gall stones, irritable bowel disease, constipation, diarrhea, GERD (reflux), pancreatitis, etc.

Training: Medical school (4 yrs), internal medicine or pediatrics residency (3 yrs), gastroenterology fellowship (3-4 yrs).

Practice type: Office based primarily with both group (small) and solo-practices common. This is heavily procedure-based specialty with the bulk of the testing being performed in the hospital or surgical/endoscopy center setting.

Technology: EMR, practice management (billing & office management) system, specialty laboratory and blood testing equipment, X-ray machine (possible). If part of a large, multi-specialty practice or group setting there may be more diagnostic equipment or affiliation with an imaging center.

For more information: http://www.gastro.org/

6. Geriatrics

Specialty Description: Geriatrics can be a focus for interested internists, and family practitioners or a recognized subspecialty of internal medicine. It deals specifically with the issues pertaining to the aged and infirmed.

Sub types/related fields: Most every medical and surgical discipline has specific areas of focus for geriatrics. Gerontology is the study of the aging process itself and is a different specialty than geriatrics.

Recognizable diseases: All diseases can become more challenging and complex in the aged.

Training: Medical school (4 yrs), internal medicine or family practice residency (3 yrs), geriatrics fellowship (1-2 yrs).

Practice type: Office based primarily with both group and solo-practices common.

Technology: EMR, practice management (billing & office management) system, specialty laboratory and blood testing equipment, X-ray machine (possible). If part of a large, multi-specialty practice or group setting there may be more diagnostic equipment or affiliation with an imaging center.

For more information: http://www.americangeriatrics.org/

7. Hematology & Oncology

Specialty Description: Hematologists deal primarily with diseases (malignant and otherwise) of the blood and blood forming organs. Specialists come from both the pediatric and internal medicine ranks. Oncologists, like their hematology colleagues, can treat either children or adults and deal specifically with cancer.

Sub types/related fields: Pediatric and adult hematologists & oncologists, surgical oncology, radiation oncology (using radiation modalities to treat cancer), gynecology-oncology, neuro-oncology.

Recognizable diseases: Cancer (of any type), lymphoma, leukemia, tumors, etc.

Training: Medical school (4 yrs), residency in internal medicine or pediatrics (3 yrs), fellowship in hematology/oncology (3-5 yrs).

Practice type: Office based primarily with both group and solo-practices common.

Technology: EMR, practice management (billing & office management) system, specialty laboratory and blood testing equipment, X-ray machine (possible). If part of a large, multi-specialty practice or group setting there may be more diagnostic equipment or affiliation with an imaging center.

For more information: http://www.hematology.org/, http://www.asco.org/

8. Infectious Disease

Specialty Description: Infectious disease physicians treat a wide variety of illnesses caused as a result of biological pathogens infecting a host. Diseases can be both transmissible and communicable.

Sub types/related fields: Travel medicine, AIDS/HIV

Recognizable Diseases: HIV/AIDS, influenza, yellow fever, Ebola virus, syphilis, surgical wound infections, tetanus, botulism, etc.

Training: Medical school (4 yrs), residency in internal medicine or pediatrics (3 yrs), fellowship in infectious disease (2-3 yrs).

Practice type: Office based primarily with both group (small) and solo-practices common. Affiliation with larger hospitals or academic centers is also common.

Technology: EMR, practice management (billing & office management) system, specialty laboratory and blood testing equipment, X-ray machine (possible). If part of a large, multi-specialty practice or group setting there may be more diagnostic equipment or affiliation with an imaging center.

For more information: http://www.idsociety.org/Index.aspx

9. Internal Medicine

Specialty Description: Internal medicine specialists (internists) are the physicians for adults. They usually serve as the primary care giver for their patients and are responsible for the diagnosis and treatment of a broad range of diseases.

Sub types/related fields: Multiple subspecialties for internal medicine are available (and are listed herein).

Recognizable diseases: Internists can become involved in the treatment of almost any illness or disease encountered by their adult patients.

Training: medical school (4 yrs), internal medicine residency (3 yrs).

Practice type: Office based primarily with both group (small) and solo-practices common. Affiliation with larger hospitals or academic centers is also common.

Technology: EMR, practice management (billing & office management) system, specialty laboratory and blood testing equipment, Xray machine (possible). If part of a large, multi-specialty practice or group setting there may be more diagnostic equipment or affiliation with an imaging center.

For more information: http://www.abim.org/

10. Nephrology

Specialty Description: Nephrologists deal with diseases of the kidneys and can be focused on either adults or children.

Sub types/related fields: Diabetology, critical (intensive) care, transplant nephrology, dialysis.

Recognizable Diseases: Hypertension (high blood pressure), renal failure, electrolyte disturbances, dialysis dependency.

Training: Medical school (4 yrs), residency in internal medicine or pediatrics (3 yrs), fellowship in nephrology (2-4 yrs).

Practice type: Office based primarily with both group (small) and solo-practices common. Affiliation with larger hospitals, academic and/or dialysis centers are also common.

Technology: EMR, practice management (billing & office management) system, specialty laboratory and blood testing equipment, X-ray machine (possible). If part of a large, multi-specialty practice or group setting there may be more diagnostic equipment or affiliation with an imaging center. Often have standalone dialysis centers.

For more information: http://www.asn-online.org/

11. Neurology

Specialty Description: Neurologists deal with diseases of the brain and nervous system.

Sub types/related fields: Neuropsychiatry.

Recognizable diseases: Epilepsy, stroke, seizures, ALS (Lou Gehrig's disease), myasthenia gravis, etc.

Training: Medical school (4 yrs), internship in internal medicine (1 yr), residency in neurology (3 yrs), fellowship (1-2 yrs) optional.

Practice type: Office based primarily with both group (small) and solo-practices common. Affiliation with larger hospitals, academic and/or neurosurgical centers are also common.

Technology: EMR, practice management (billing & office management) system, specialty laboratory and blood testing equipment, X-ray machine (possible). If part of a large, multi-specialty practice or group setting there may be more diagnostic equipment or affiliation with an imaging center. CT, MRI, angiography, etc. may be used as well; often in the hospital setting.

For more information: http://www.aneuroa.org/

12. Occupational Health

Specialty Description: Occupational Health is a unique field of medicine that deals with helping to protect the health, safety and welfare of workers engaged in various activities.

Sub types/related fields: Aerospace medicine, flight surgeon (military) diving medicine, occupational medicine, occupational (or industrial) hygiene, public health, safety engineering / industrial engineering, chemistry, health physics.

Recognizable Diseases: Injury prevention.

Training: Medical school (4 yrs), variable education following medical school.

Practice type: Office based primarily with both group (small) and solo-practices common. Affiliation with larger hospitals, academic centers, certain industries or governmental agencies is also common.

Technology: EMR, practice management (billing & office management) system, specialty laboratory and blood testing equipment, X-ray machine (possible). If part of a large, multi-specialty practice or group setting there may be more diagnostic equipment or affiliation with an imaging center.

For more information: http://www.osha.gov/

13. Pediatrics

Specialty Description: Pediatricians deal with diseases of infants, children and young adults. They are considered the primary care provider for this age group. Like their adult counterparts (internists), pediatricians can diagnose and treat a myriad of illnesses.

Sub types/related fields: Many subspecialties are available for pediatricians. They are similar to the adult subspecialties.

Recognizable Diseases: Pediatricians can become involved in the treatment of almost any illness or disease encountered by their young patients.

Training: Medical school (4 yrs), residency in pediatrics (3 yrs).

Practice type: Office based primarily with both group (small) and solo-practices common. Affiliation with larger hospitals or academic centers is also common.

Technology: EMR, practice management (billing & office management) system, specialty laboratory and blood testing equipment, X-ray machine (possible). If part of a large, multi-specialty practice or group setting there may be more diagnostic equipment or affiliation with an imaging center.

For more information: https://www.abp.org/

14. Pulmonology & Critical Care

Specialty Description: Pulmonologists deal primarily with diseases of the lungs and respiratory system. Critical care physicians are involved mainly in the hospital setting and often are in charge of overseeing the intensive care units, handling complex ventilation management and coordinating care of the most critical patients.

Sub types/related fields: Sleep medicine, intensivist (critical care specialist).

Recognizable Diseases: Pneumonia, asthma, tuberculosis, emphysema, and complicated chest infections.

Training: Medical school (4yrs), internal medicine residency (3 yrs), fellowship in pulmonology & critical care (2-4 yrs).

Practice type: Office based primarily with both group and solo-practices common. Affiliation with larger hospitals and academic centers is also common.

Technology: EMR, practice management (billing & office management) system, specialty laboratory and blood testing equipment, X-ray machine, CT scanners, PET scanners (possible). If part of a large, multi-specialty practice or group setting there may be more diagnostic equipment or affiliation with an imaging center.

The majority of their testing and imagery is located in hospital settings. Invasive procedures (bronchoscopy) are performed in hospital settings.

For more information: http://www.lung.org/

15. Rehabilitation Medicine (Physiatry)

Physiatrists care for sick or injured patients and attempt to help restore their functionality, performance and quality of life.

Sub types/related fields: Sports medicine, pain management, hospice/ palliative care, spinal cord injury.

Recognizable Diseases: Severe arthritis, paralysis (traumatic, post-surgical, accidental, etc.), sports injuries, end of life care, comfort care situations.

Training: Medical school (4yrs), residency in rehabilitative medicine (3-4 yrs).

Practice type: Office or hospital based with both group (small) and solo-practices common. Affiliation with larger hospitals, academic and/or neurosurgical, rehabilitation centers and/or nursing homes/extended care facilities is also common.

Technology: EMR, practice management (billing & office management) system, specialty laboratory and blood testing equipment, X-ray machine (possible). If part of a large, multi-specialty practice or group setting there may be more diagnostic equipment or affiliation with an imaging center. CT, MRI, angiography, etc. may be used as well; often in the hospital setting.

For more information: http://www.aapmr.org/

16. Rheumatology

Specialty Description: Rheumatologists deal mainly with clinical problems involving joints, soft tissues, autoimmune diseases, vasculitis, and other heritable connective tissue disorders. They can work closely with other specialties in the medical and surgical fields.

Sub types/related fields: None.

Recognizable Diseases: Gout, rheumatoid arthritis, lupus, scleroderma, vasculitis, sarcoidosis.

Training: Medical school (4yrs), residency in rheumatology (3-4 yrs).

Practice type: Office or hospital based with both group (small) and solo-practices common. Affiliation with larger hospitals, academic and/or neurosurgical, rehabilitation centers and/or nursing homes/extended care facilities is also common.

Technology: EMR, practice management (billing & office management) system, specialty laboratory and blood testing equipment, Xray machine (possible). If part of a large, multi-specialty practice or group setting there may be more diagnostic equipment or affiliation with an imaging center. CT, MRI, angiography, etc. may be used as well; often in the hospital setting.

For more information: http://www.rheumatology.org/

THE SURGICAL SPECIALTIES

The surgical specialties have their basic roots in general surgery and are classically differentiated from medical specialties due to their training, philosophy and intensive reliance on invasive surgical testing and procedures as a method of treatment, although in today's modern medical environment, many medical specialties perform extensive procedures as well.

Most, if not all surgical specialties, because of their reliance on specific equipment and highly trained staff are predominantly hospital (or surgery center) based. Surgeons do spend time in the office as that is where many post-operative patients go for follow up. Minor surgical procedures are still performed in the office settings. Some surgical offices, depending on the specialty, will have specialized testing and diagnostic equipment as well as an EMR, practice management and billing capabilities.

Sales personnel who call predominantly on surgeons with generally include specialized equipment vendors, biotechnology manufacturers, pharmaceutical representatives, IT and managed services providers and financial service representatives.

Surgical practices traditionally have been made up of smaller groups or solo practitioners. However, with the changes being seen in medicine more and more surgeons are banding together into larger groups.

Training to become a surgeon is difficult and similar in scope to other specialties. Students first must complete a four year medical school followed by a residency and fellowship depending. The length of each is dependent on the specialty and individual program requirements. Some programs require the completion of a general surgery residency (5 yrs) before enrolling in a fellowship program while other programs will bundle the residency and fellowship into a single program type. Overall training for most surgical subspecialties is 5 to 9 years after medical school.

Further information can be found: http://www.facs.org/

Surgical Specialty Definitions

1. General Surgery - General surgeons diagnose and treat basic surgical diseases and injuries. Common diseases they treat include organ biopsies, minor trauma, thyroid disease, hernias, etc. Subspecialties of general surgery include colorectal surgery, gastrointestinal surgery, trauma surgery, and transplant surgery.

http://www.theasgs.org/

2. Cardiovascular & Thoracic Surgery - Cardiovascular & thoracic surgeons treat diseases and injury to the chest, lungs, heart and vasculature in the chest area. Diseases they frequently encounter are advanced coronary artery disease, advanced valvular heart disease, lung cancer, esophageal disorders, and severe chest trauma.

http://www.aats.org/

3. ENT (Otolaryngology) - Also commonly referred to as "ear, nose and throat" surgeons or "head & neck" surgeons, otolaryngologists deal with diseases and trauma to the head and neck. Problems they frequently encounter include trauma, malignancies, and reconstructions.

http://www.entnet.org/

4. Neurosurgery - Neurosurgeons treat illnesses and injury to the brain and nervous system. Problems frequently encountered include head trauma, paralysis, spinal injury, brain tumors,

http://www.aans.org/

5. Orthopedic (& Spine) Surgery - Orthopedic surgeons treat illness and injuries to the skeletal system. Problems frequently encountered include severe skeletal trauma, malignancies, amputations, severe arthritis. Subspecialties of orthopedic surgery include hand surgery, trauma surgery, joint replacement, sports injury and spinal surgery.

http://www.aaos.org/

6. Oral & Maxillofacial Surgery - This surgical subspecialty deals with illness, disease and trauma to the face and mouth.

http://www.aaoms.org/

7. Plastic & Reconstructive Surgery - This surgical subspecialty deals with restoration and repair of damaged areas of the body secondary to disease, injury, trauma or previous surgery. Plastic surgeons often deal with elective (or voluntary) alteration, restoration or repair of various body parts such as the face, breasts, skin, etc.

http://www.plasticsurgery.org/
http://www.cosmeticsurgery.org/
http://www.surgery.org/
http://www.aafprs.org/
http://www.aaps1921.org/

8. Vascular Surgery - Vascular surgeons deal with injury and diseases of the vascular system. Problems frequently encountered include severe vascular trauma, malignancy with vascular involvement, vascular disease requiring bypass (non-cardiac).

http://www.theasgs.org/,
http://www.facs.org/about/councils/advvasc/advvasc.html

THE HYBRID SPECIALTIES

The hybrid specialties are those that combine elements of both medicine and surgery or are so unique in that they don't easily fit into either category. The most common of these specialties are:

1. Anesthesiology

Specialty Description: Anesthesiologists deal with the administration of anesthesia and the monitoring of patients before, during and for a period of time after specific procedures such as surgeries and specific diagnostic and therapeutic tests. Providers other than physicians, such as nurse anesthetists and their assistants can administer certain anesthetic agents also.

Sub types/related fields: None.

Recognizable Diseases: Anesthesiologists can become involved in the treatment of any disease where the administration of anesthesia is a necessary part of the care plan.

Training: Medical school (4 yrs), residency in anesthesia (4 yrs). Certified Nurse Anesthetists (CNA) have a separate training process.

Practice type: May be solo or group practice, but hospital based primarily.

Technology: The equipment they use, including EMRs and practice support items, are generally provided by the hospitals in which they practice.

For more information: http://www.asahq.org/

2. Dermatology

Specialty Description: Dermatologists deal primarily with diseases of the skin, including cosmetic problems with the hair, scalp and nails. It is a hybrid specialty in that physicians encompass both medical and surgical techniques in the care of their patients.

Sub types/related fields: Cosmetic dermatology, dermatopathology, immunodermatology.

Recognizable Diseases: Psoriasis, moles, skin cancer, rash, etc.

Training: Medical school (4 yrs), internal medicine internship (1 yr.), dermatology fellowship (3 yrs).

Practice type: Office primarily with both group and solo-practices common.

Technology: EMR, practice management (billing & office management) system, specialty laboratory and blood testing equipment, X-ray machine (possible). If part of a large, multi-specialty practice or group setting there may be more diagnostic equipment or affiliation with an imaging center.

For more information: http://www.aad.org/

3. Emergency Medicine

Specialty Description: Emergency physicians staff the emergency departments of most hospitals and are responsible for at the immediate diagnosis and stabilization of many moderate and critically ill or injured patients. Many patients with various other types of less acute problems present to the emergency department as well and emergency physicians are likely to diagnose, treat then release these individuals to follow up care with their community providers.

Sub types/related fields: None.

Recognizable Diseases: Emergency physicians see "anything that walks into the door."

Training: Medical school (4 yrs), residency in emergency medicine (3 yrs), certain fellowships are available (1-2 yrs).

Practice type: May be solo or group practice, but hospital based primarily.

Technology: The equipment they use, including EMRs and practice support items, are generally provided by the hospitals in which they practice.

For more information: http://www.acep.org/, http://www.aaem.org/

4. Obstetrics & Gynecology

Specialty Description: ObGyns provide care to pregnant women throughout the course of pregnancy; including delivery and the immediate postpartum period. They also deal with illness and disease exclusive to women and women's health.

Sub types/related fields: Maternal-Fetal Medicine, Gynecology-oncology.

Recognizable Diseases: All issues related to pregnancy, women's health and reproduction.

Training: Medical school (4 yrs), residency in obstetrics & gynecology (4 yrs), certain fellowships are available (1-3 yrs).

Practice type: May be solo or group practice. Hospital based primarily for deliveries. Office activities are common also.

Technology: EMR, practice management (billing & office management) system, specialty laboratory and blood testing equipment, X-ray machine (possible). If part of a large, multi-specialty practice or group setting there may be more diagnostic equipment or affiliation with an imaging center. CT, MRI, angiography, etc. may be used as well; often in the hospital setting.

For more information: http://www.acog.org/

5. Ophthalmology

Specialty Description: Ophthalmologists deal with the diagnosis and treatment of diseases and trauma to the eye.

Sub types/related fields: Multiple subspecialties are available including cornea, glaucoma, cataract, neuro-ophthalmology and ocular oncology.

Recognizable Diseases: Cataracts, glaucoma, corneal injury, retinal detachment, "floaters," eye trauma.

Training: Medical School (4 yrs), residency in ophthalmology (4 years), specific fellowships are available (1-3 yrs).

Practice type: May be solo or group practice. Hospital based primarily for surgeries. Office activities are common also.

Technology: EMR, practice management (billing & office management) system, specialty laboratory and blood testing equipment, X-ray machine (possible). If part of a large, multi-specialty practice or group setting there may be more diagnostic equipment or affiliation with an imaging center. CT, MRI, angiography, etc. may be used as well; often in the hospital setting.

For more information: http://www.aao.org/

6. Pathology

Specialty Description: Pathologists use specific tests and equipment to make critical diagnoses and aid with treatment. Pathological specimens are obtained from routine blood tests, biopsies and other surgical and other diagnostic procedures.

Sub types/related fields: Pathologists can specialize in many different areas.

Recognizable Diseases: Pathologists can encounter many, if not all, diseases throughout the course of their practices. Most common activities include differentiating malignant from non-malignant tumors and lesions.

Training: Medical School (4 yrs), residency in pathology (3-4 yrs), fellowships are available (1-3 yrs).

Practice type: May be solo or group practice. Hospital based primarily.

Technology: The equipment they use, including EMRs and practice support items, are generally provided by the hospitals in which they practice.

For more information: http://www.ascp.org/, http://www.cap.org/apps/cap.portal

7. Radiology

Specialty Description: Radiologists use many types of imaging technologies (such as x-ray radiography, ultrasound (USN), computed tomography (CT), nuclear medicine, positron emission tomography (PET) and magnetic resonance imaging (MRI) to diagnose and/or treat diseases. Interventional radiologists perform invasive medical procedures with the guidance of imaging technologies to assist with patient care.

Sub types/related fields: Many areas of specialty are available to radiologists such as diagnostic and interventional radiology which are the most common.

Training: Medical school (4 yrs), residency in radiology (4 yrs), fellowships are available (1-3 yrs).

Practice type: May be solo or group practice. Hospital based primarily.

Technology: The equipment they use, including EMRs and practice support items, are generally provided by the hospitals in which they practice.

For more information: http://www.acr.org/

SUMMARY

Understanding that all physicians are not created equal, don't practice equally or need your goods and services equally is an important first step in successfully selling into the healthcare market. The above information introduces the basics about your physician customers and lays a foundation for you to begin to approach your accounts. Building accurate and efficient account profiles is necessary for successful selling. The information presented herein will set you on a proper course to making that happen. Good luck.

Made in the USA
Monee, IL
14 November 2026

68512946R00125